Foreword

Glasgow has long since lost its title of Second City of the British Empire. Even with the population halved, it is so much better for this. Industrial preeminence brought with it a high price in pollution, grime and wretched housing conditions. With the heavy industry gone, Britain's finest Victorian city has scrubbed up nicely. More of its architecture could have been saved, but equally, it has lost a lot of failed 'development' that it needed losing.

The city centre has been reclaimed as a space for living as well as commerce. Beautiful redundant buildings – especially fabulous churches with no congregations – have been transformed into theatres, music venues, visual arts hubs, restaurants and even an indoor mountain for rock climbing. The citizenry has also scrubbed up well. The paradigm shift is towards fit, fashionable, tobacco-free, sober and in possession of your own teeth.

What has not changed is Glasgow's creativity, in music, art, drama, literature and humour. Raw energy spills over into daily life; the city knows how to party. Asking a local for directions is a good way to get the full flavour of Glasgow – though the local accent is famously raw. If confused, simply ask, 'Gonnae gie's that again, pal?' ('Would you please repeat that?')

Cuisine has improved immensely. Dining out used to mean fish and chips consumed in a bus shelter. Now the norm is eclectic and international, with a strong focus on Scotland's excellent natural produce, in a huge variety of restaurants housed in charming locations. The city founded on religion has long had a reputation for unsavoury conflict between the two flavours of Christianity. Aside from the behaviour of some followers of its two big football clubs, this is also changing.

After a period of post-industrial angst, Glaswegians have learned to proclaim their love for Scotland's first city – a love that has proved contagious among its legions of visitors.

Tom Shields

111 Places
in Glasgow
That You
Shouldn't Miss

Photographs by Gillian Tait

111 Places

© Emons Verlag GmbH
All rights reserved
© Photographs: © Gillian Tait except:
Braehead Curling (ch. 16), photo supplied by intu Braehead;
Carbeth Huts (ch. 22), photo: Sharon Stewart; Glasgow's Dalí (ch. 48),
top photo © CSG CIC Glasgow Museums Collection;
Kelvingrove Bandstand (ch. 60), photo supplied by Page\Park, © Andrew Lee;
The Whangie (ch. 110), photo: Sharon Stewart
© Cover motif: Mauritius images/David Robertson/Alamy
Edited by Gillian Tait
Printing and binding: Lensing Druck GmbH & Co. KG,
Feldbachacker 16, 44149 Dortmund
Design: Eva Kraskes, based on a design
by Lübbeke | Naumann | Thoben
Maps: altancicek.design, www.altancicek.de
Printed in Germany 2018
ISBN 978-3-7408-0256-1
First edition

Did you enjoy it? Do you want more?
Join us in uncovering new places around the world on:
www.111places.com

1 1 La Belle Place

Architecture for architecture's sake

Why settle for a mere portrait on canvas when the façade of a beautiful building can be used as a postcard to posterity? Glasgow merchant David Bell had this in mind when in 1857 he decreed the creation of a refined pleasure dome called the Queen's Rooms. Its purpose remains not entirely clear, apart from being a venue where leaders of trade, commerce and industry might gather to discuss art and the finer things in life. A measure of freemasonry was also involved.

The original interior no longer exists, but the exterior tells its own story, with its elaborate frieze and esoteric imagery celebrating 'the progress of the arts'. The orchestrator of this performance in stone, architect Charles Wilson, is depicted on the entrance façade handing over the plans to his client's wife. Mrs Bell is personified as Minerva, goddess of arts sponsorship. The frieze continues round the side where it is accompanied by a row of carved heads in medallions, whose cast list reveals a measure of self-indulgence. John Mossman, designer of the frieze and godfather of Glasgow monumental sculpture, is featured, and his assistant, stonecarver Walter Buchan, also gets a look in. David Hamilton, mentor to Wilson, is another who gets a heads up. The rear of the Queen's Rooms is plain but occupies La Belle Allée, surely the coolest street name in the city.

Look away to the lofty town houses of Park Circus, another exemplar of Charles Wilson's legacy. He drafted the plans for the exclusive Park District in the 1850s, when wealthy Glaswegians decided to abandon the city centre and go west.

After it ceased to be a club for culture cognoscenti, the Queen's Rooms went on to have other interesting occupants. It became a Christian Science church, and is currently home to the Om Hindu Mandir. In its own way, the colourful interior of this temple matches the exuberance of Mr Bell's palace of art.

Address 1 La Belle Place, G3 7LH, +44 (0)141 332 0482, www.hindumandirglasgow.org |
Getting there Buses 3, 17, 77, X76 to Elderslie Street | Hours Exterior accessible 24 hours;
Hindu Mandir: Mon–Sat 9.30am–12.30pm & 4.30–7.30pm, Sun 10.30am–2.30pm | Tip
Cultivate inner peace with a lunchtime meditation class at Vajrayana Kadampa Buddhist
Centre (5 Bentinck Street, G3 7SB, +44 (0)141 334 1334, Mon–Fri 1.15–1.45pm; evening
classes also available).

2 7 Arches

Windows into Gorbals history

Gorbals used to be famous as a haven for Europe's huddled masses, and infamous for the violence of its razor gangs, notoriously portrayed in the 1935 novel *No Mean City*. Only memories of these days remain, and a mere handful of its old buildings survive. The rest, superior and squalid alike, were obliterated as if Gorbals was just a stain on the map rather than a once vibrant community.

A little slice of Gorbals history has recently been depicted in an artwork under a disused railway bridge. Like altars of remembrance, its arches are dedicated to the stories of three of many notable natives. Allan Pinkerton emigrated to the USA, and in 1849 was appointed Chicago's first police detective. As head of military intelligence for the Union side in the American Civil War, he worked closely with Abraham Lincoln. He went on to form the Pinkerton Detective Agency, pursuing bank robbers such as Jesse James and Butch Cassidy.

Benny Lynch was just 22 when he became Scotland's first world boxing champion. He was only 33 when he died, losing his fight against alcoholism. The last of the trio is artist Hannah Frank, daughter of emigré Russian-Jewish parents, known for her individual drawings in Art Nouveau style. She later turned to sculpture, and lived to the age of 100. Among other Gorbals people who have made their mark but as yet have no memorial are Thomas Lipton, the self-made millionaire grocer, most famous for tea and for never winning the America's Cup yacht race, Alexander Watson Hutton, known as the father of Argentinian football, and more recently footballer and pundit Paddy Crerand.

A plan is afoot to recreate the decorative fountain and clock that formerly stood at Gorbals Cross, and was bulldozed for no good reason. An exact replica of the fountain exists on the Caribbean island of St Kitts and Nevis. A copy of this copy may soon again adorn Gorbals.

Address Cleland Street Underpass, G5 0TS | Getting there Buses 5, 6, 7, 7A, 21, 31, 267 to Gorbals Street | Tip Just across the wasteland from the arches, at 170 Gorbals Street, stands the British Linen Bank building, neglected but potentially lovely. This last surviving Gorbals tenement of note is shortly to be restored to its original 1900 eminence.

3 The ABC

A mover and shaker of the movies

In its present incarnation, the O2 ABC is one of Glasgow's most dynamic music venues, with concerts by emerging artists and a varied club agenda. This vast warehouse of noise and fun has a diverse and exotic history. Built in 1875 as the Diorama, which displayed huge canvases of historic events, it later became Hubner's Ice-Skating Palace. A hint of its future came in May 1896, when it was used for Glasgow's very first public film show. In the early 20th century it became the Hippodrome, home of Hengler's Circus, with films shown in the off season. In 1929 it was converted for the Associated British Film Corporation into the Regal, a flagship 2,359-seater cinema.

In a way, this building is a memorial to John Maxwell, the founder of the original ABC chain, who was described in his *Times* obituary in 1940 as 'the most outstanding personality in the British film industry'. Born in 1879 in Cambuslang, Maxwell was the son of a butcher. He became a lawyer, and an astute businessman with an interest in cinema. In 1912 he purchased a picturehouse in Glasgow, which developed into a chain of 20 cinemas, and in 1925 he moved to London to take over the Wardour Films distribution company. Among the major foreign films he brought to British audiences was Fritz Lang's *Metropolis*.

Maxwell soon moved into production, with British International Pictures at Elstree Studios. In his canny way he declared, 'There will be no foolish expenditure, enough money will be spent to do any subject chosen justice.' He nurtured unknown talent, notably Alfred Hitchcock, with the groundbreaking talkie *Blackmail* (1929). Maxwell was a hands-on producer, but his main interest was in building up a company that combined making films and distributing them with owning cinemas. With 500 upmarket screens, his Associated British Cinemas was second in the world only to Fox West Coast in the USA.

Address 300 Sauchiehall Street, G2 3JA, see www.academymusicgroup.com/o2abcglasgow for details of the music programme | Getting there Buses 3, 4, 4A, 15, 17, 77 to Pitt Street; subway to Cowcaddens; train to Charing Cross | Tip Should you wish to catch a good movie today, the Glasgow Film Theatre is nearby at 12 Rose Street, G3 6RB. Built in Art Deco style in 1939 as an arthouse cinema, it still thrives as an independent institution showing a mix of classic, contemporary and world film, with a nice café and bar (www.glasgowfilm.org).

4__ The Arboretum
Tree-spotting in the Botanics

On a visit to the Botanic Gardens, you will want to wander around the glasshouses and enjoy their collection of some 10,000 exotic and colourful plants, from beautiful orchids and begonias to devilish, insectivorous Venus Fly Traps. But you should also make time for the tree trail. This takes in the top 20 trees in the Botanics, most of which are to be found in the Arboretum, located in a quiet corner near the Kirklee gate. A leaflet is available with a map and details of the individual trees in this rare collection from all over the world, gathered by plant hunters over the two centuries of the Botanics' history.

Seek out the small but perfect Paperbark Maple. Of Chinese origin, its name comes from its coppery-cinnamon bark, which peels into translucent swirls. In autumn, the bright green leaves transform into a riot of pink and vibrant red. Other immigrants include the Moroccan Fir, also known as the Hedgehog Tree because of its prickly leaves, and the Monkey Puzzle, a stunning remnant of prehistoric times. It originated in Chile where, ironically, there are no monkeys to puzzle. Go native and find the Scottish Whitebeam, which grows wild only on the Isle of Arran, and is Scotland's rarest tree. It has rugged Scottish characteristics: it is not very tall, preferring to keep low in remote valleys, away from high winds and the worst of the weather.

After the tree trail and a stroll along the River Kelvin walkway, the visitor will no doubt wish to chill out (or, more accurately, warm up) in the tropical ambience of the Kibble Palace, the Botanics' jewel of a glasshouse. There is a traditional Scottish tearoom next door.

In its early days, the Botanics was the preserve of the wealthy, who paid a yearly subscription of one guinea (£1.05). The poor were admitted only on occasional open days, on payment of one old penny. Admission is now free.

Address Botanic Gardens, 730 Great Western Road, G12 0UE, +44 (0)141 276 1614, www.glasgowbotanicgardens.com | **Getting there** Buses 6, 6A, 6B, 8, 8A, 10A, 90, 372 to Botanic Gardens; subway to Hillhead | **Hours** Arboretum: daily 7am–dusk; glasshouses: 10am–6pm (4.15pm in winter) | **Tip** Try to catch one of the Gardens' many summer events: a concert, open-air film show, or a Shakespeare play during the Bard in the Botanics season.

5 — The Arlington Baths

A place of health and beauty

A private members' swimming club founded in 1870, the Arlington is the oldest institution of its kind in the world. The A-listed building has more than a hint of the Roman bathhouse, in a solid Glaswegian way. So successful was the Arlington set-up that an exact replica was soon built in London.

The sunlit pool, with its trapeze and Tarzanesque swing ropes, offers both gentle and vigorous exercise. The ambience of the club is typified by the darkly seductive Turkish room. Steam rooms, saunas, big slipper baths and cool rooms add to the relaxation and comfort. But the Arlington has changed with the times. In its earlier days its healthy pursuits were countered by the provision of poolside ashtrays for swimmers to pause for a cigarette. The wooden-beamed billiards room has now been transformed into a gym with the latest equipment. And it no longer employs a 'pants boy' to collect discarded swimwear.

The Arlington has a place in history as the pool where water polo was invented, and developed into an Olympic sport, by William Wilson, its first baths master and a major figure in the promotion of aquatic exercise. 'Water rugby' was how the sport was first described, but it also involved wrestling, dive-bombing by the goalkeeper, and holding opponents underwater to recover the ball. Water polo is less rough now, but it's still a lively sport that Glasgow can be proud of.

A few decades ago, with dwindling membership, the Arlington faced a crisis merely to preserve the fine building. Volunteers rose to the challenge and sparked off a renaissance, not only securing the fabric but also updating all the facilities sensitively, in keeping with the original ethos. It is a private club, but anyone with an interest can arrange a free tour, sample the facilities for a fee, or visit on an open day. Recent special events have included an underwater light and sound experience.

Address 61 Arlington Street, G3 6DT, +44 (0)141 332 6021, www.arlingtonbaths.co.uk | **Getting there** Buses 4, 4A, 15 to Lynedoch Street; subway to St George's Cross | **Hours** Members only; check website for details of tours, open days and special events | **Tip** The Park Circus area across Woodlands Road is well worth a stroll around, to have a look at some of Glasgow's grandest town houses and other fine 19th-century architecture.

6 Auchentoshan Distillery
The spirit of Glasgow

Most Scotch whisky makers make much of locations in Highland glens, on heather-clad hillsides, or nestling on the coasts of Hebridean islands. Just 12 miles to the west of Glasgow, however, is a distillery that is determinedly proud of its connection with the city. Auchentoshan – the Gaelic name means 'corner of the field' – was 'forged in the fires of the Industrial Revolution and the sweat of our Glaswegian forefathers,' as its publicity boasts. It hastens to add, 'We've taken the sweat out now. But boy, do we still have the spirit.' Auchentoshan whisky is unique in that it is all triple-distilled. It has been described as the 'breakfast whisky' because of its sweet, clean taste – though the practice of having a dram with your morning porridge has largely died out.

The distillery has quite a rural appearance, a whitewashed cluster set in fields off the road to Loch Lomond. Whisky has been made here for centuries, though legally only since 1823. It is only a few miles from Clydebank, a former hive of shipbuilding and engineering that was severely bombed during World War II. A warehouse at Auchentoshan received a direct hit, resulting in a spectacular river of blazing whisky. But the story that a stray bomb created the hollow that holds the water used to cool down the distilling process is an urban myth. The crater involved in the production of the *cratur* (an old Scots-Irish word for whisky) predates the Blitz.

Auchentoshan offers a variety of visitor experiences, from a one-hour tour with a dram to master classes and tutored tastings. Learn all about the malting, milling and mashing of the barley, the mixing with pure Loch Katrine water, the triple distillation, and the ageing in a variety of bourbon, sherry and fine-wine oak casks. The guides will answer all the queries that a whisky buff might have, apart from the traditional, frequently-asked Glasgow question, 'Whose turn is it to buy a round?'

Address Great Western Road, Clydebank, G81 4SJ, +44 (0)1389 878561, www.auchentoshan.com | **Getting there** Train to Dalmuir, then bus 1D to Kimberley Street and a 5-minute walk | **Hours** Daily 10am–5pm; see website for information on tours and prices | **Tip** The Clydeside Distillery is a modern single malt distillery, with a café and specialist shop, recently opened at The Old Pumphouse, Queen's Dock, 100 Stobcross Road, G3 8QQ (daily 10am–4pm, tours on the hour, www.theclydeside.com).

7 _ The Barras

Where BAaD is good

Glasgow's huge and famous Barras – a flea market that never called itself a flea market – has been in gradual decline due to changing shopping habits. Now it is being revitalised, thanks to a hipster transplant. A younger generation has moved into some of the empty spaces and created Barras Art and Design (BAaD), bringing in a new customer base.

First some history. Back in the early 20th century an enterprising young woman called Maggie McIver, who began her working life on a fruit stall in the East End, had the idea of renting out barrows to traders at a weekend market. The Barras (local pronunciation of 'barrows') grew into a commercial giant with 18 different markets, 1,000 stalls and 150 shops. The poor and not so poor flocked for bargains in clothing, food, furniture and just about every item for the home. Many of those traders are now gone, but there remains a profusion of second-hand stalls selling bric-a-brac, or 'antiques', as many vendors prefer to call their wares.

The Barras unfortunately became infamous when honest traders were infiltrated by sellers of counterfeit and black market goods. There is still a hint of the illicit, and visitors may be approached by ambulant salesmen whispering 'tobacco' or 'Viagra'.

BAaD and the many creative businesses it has encouraged are based in the Barras Centre, a pleasant domed building. It has an upscale restaurant majoring in seafood, with lobster at up to £50, in comparison to the traditional Barras fare of mussels at £1.50 a portion. The Backyard bar and food venue attracts a young crowd, especially to live music events. In true Barras style, BAaD is a bustling marketplace, with arts and crafts alongside the bric-a-brac, merchandise that is now referred to as 'retro' or 'collectable'. One of its regular events is the Glasgow Vintage and Flea Market. The flea has finally become a selling point.

Address Between Gallowgate and London Road, G1 5AX, www.theglasgowbarras.com; Barras Centre: 54 Calton Entry, G40 2SB, www.baadglasgow.com | **Getting there** Buses 2, 60, 60A, 61, 240, 255 to Ross Street | **Hours** Barras Market: Sat & Sun 10am–5pm; BAaD: Wed–Sat noon–midnight, Sun 11am–10pm | **Tip** Most of the nearby bars are mainly for customers of a Celtic persuasion (the football club that is, not the ancient culture). An exception is The Hielan Jessie at 374 Gallowgate, a traditional pub although it opened only about 30 years ago. Jessie was a local lassie who was apparently not unfamiliar with the soldiers from a nearby barracks.

8___ Barrowland Ballroom
Ziggy's pocketful of stardust

In the 1980s, the grand era of the Glasgow dance hall was over, and the famous Barrowland Ballroom faced an uncertain future. It was saved when local band Simple Minds chose this place of unforgotten dreams as the backdrop for a video. The music industry realised it was a unique concert venue, and Barrowland was given a new lease of life. The barrelled ceiling made for great acoustics. The Glasgow audiences contributed atmosphere and a bit of edgy intimacy in the 1,900-capacity hall. Irish singer Christy Moore declared Barrowland his favourite venue, adding that it was 'not for the faint-hearted'. Moore is not alone in his admiration. Arctic Monkeys and Alice Cooper, Blur and Blondie, Madness and Manic Street Preachers through to Amy Winehouse and The Waterboys – the alphabetical archive is a hall of fame.

When spaceman David Bowie took his *Earthling* tour there in 1997, he caught a falling star and put it in his pocket. One of the decorative stars on the ceiling fell off during the performance. Bowie purloined it, and kept it as a souvenir in the bathroom of his Paris flat. The Barrowland star then became a tradition, with the management thoughtfully decorating the dressing room with celestial facsimiles for visiting performers to steal. Scottish band Biffy Clyro made their mark by having their lyrics inscribed on the steps of Barrowland's magical staircase.

Various big music venue operators have tried to buy Barrowland, but it remains resolutely in Glaswegian hands. It was built in 1934 by legendary Barras Market founder Maggie McIver as a place to hold events for her stallholders. It soon became a hot spot for 'the jiggin', as Glaswegians called a night out at a dance hall. For three decades the resident band was Billy MacGregor and the Gaybirds. Something of a showman, Billy and his boys interspersed the music with comedy sketches. The fun continues.

Address 244 Gallowgate, G4 0TT, +44 (0)141 552 4601, www.glasgow-barrowland.com | Getting there Buses 2, 60, 60A, 61, 240, 255 to Ross Street | Hours Check website for concert dates | Tip The Scotia Bar, 112 Stockwell Street, G1 4LW, is the place for lively local music, especially on a Friday night if the Frank O'Hagan Experience is playing. This classic Glasgow boozer claims to be the city's oldest pub, as do some other contenders (+44 (0)141 552 8681).

9 The Battlefield Rest

Love on the tram

Architectural historians will have their own way of describing it, but the best word for this former tram terminus built in 1914 is simply 'cute'. Why a tram stop should need an octagonal clock tower and ornamental balcony, all clad in pretty green and white tiles, is something only its creators could explain. We do know that in Edwardian times Glasgow Corporation Transport did things in style. The Battlefield Rest became a well-loved landmark, and its waiting room was through the decades a favourite rendezvous point for courting couples.

With the closure of the Glasgow tram system in the 1960s, the Rest was relegated to the status of a big bus shelter, and the building was shamefully neglected. In the early 1980s the decision to demolish it met with wide popular protest, notably by two young women who tied themselves, suffragette-style, to the doors.

Enter Marco Giannasi, a Scots-Italian who had studied architecture in Italy but had returned to Glasgow to run his family's restaurant business. He bought the Battlefield Rest for £1 and set about the restoration. Only the granite floor was still intact. By luck, the company that supplied the original tiles still had the plans for the building. The Battlefield Rest is now an award-winning bistro specialising in Scottish and Italian produce. The balcony is home to two beehives, whose honey is used in the kitchen. Courting couples still meet at the Rest, but in rather more comfort, to partake perhaps of some smoked haddock ravioli and a glass of prosecco. A husband and wife recently travelled up from England to have dinner, to mark the 50th anniversary of their first date at the old tram terminus. Marco Giannasi is now a confirmed tram enthusiast. If plans to pedestrianise the street go ahead, he hopes to find space to park an old tramcar and convert it into a tearoom and small theatre.

Address 55 Battlefield Road, G42 9JL, +44 (0)141 636 6955, www.battlefieldrest.co.uk | Getting there Buses 4, 4A, 5, 121 to Victoria Infirmary; train to Mount Florida from Central Station | Hours Mon–Sat 10am–10pm (last orders) | Tip Tramway is the city's former tramcar works and depot, now transformed into a spacious venue for contemporary visual and performing arts, with interesting Hidden Gardens to entertain children (25 Albert Drive, G41 2PE, www.tramway.org).

10 Bearsden Bathhouse

When the Romans ruled in Scotland

It may look like a heap of old stones beside a modern apartment block but it is, in fact, part of a UNESCO World Heritage Site. These remains of a bathhouse are evidence that nearly 2,000 years ago civilised plumbing had reached what is now Scotland. The latrine in the foreground of the picture was probably the northernmost lavatory in the Roman Empire. The bathhouse was built about 120 A.D. as part of the Antonine Wall complex. The reconquest of southern Scotland was more for the greater glory of the emperor who gave the wall its name, Antoninus Pius, than for strategic value.

Though made not from stone but of timber and turf, it was a big beautiful wall, and the Romans made the local tribes pay for it through taxation and slavery. An artist's reconstruction on an information panel at the site shows that it was a comfortable enough life for the Roman legionnaires in far-flung Caledonia, with upmarket accommodation and a diet including olives, figs and wine. Not unlike Bearsden today.

Most of the 37-mile wall, from Old Kilpatrick in the west to Bo'ness in the east, is submerged under the developments of modern-day central Scotland, but there are extensive stretches where the ramparts and other remains are still visible, and accessible on a number of pleasant country walks. But to get a vivid picture of how it once was, visit the Hunterian Museum at Glasgow University, which has a permanent exhibition with a fine collection of sculpture and artefacts from the Antonine Wall. The objects – jewels, coins, leather shoes – bring to life the wealth and culture of this far outpost of the Roman Empire. Engravings of distance markers from the wall illustrate the cruelty and enslavement inflicted on the indigenous population. The local tribes fought a continual guerilla war against the occupation, which led to Rome abandoning the wall only some 25 years after it was built.

A WOODEN BENCH WITH ROUND HOLES CUT IN IT WOULD HAVE PROVIDED THE SEATING OVER THIS SEWER CHANNEL

Address Roman Road, Bearsden, G61 2SL (entrance opposite number 16) | Getting there Buses 6B, 15, 17, 118, 347 to Roman Road; train to Bearsden from Queen Street, then 8-minute walk | Hours Accessible 24 hours | Tip Café Crème, round the corner at 14 New Kirk Road, is the place Bearsden's Roman legions would have gone for coffee and cake if it had been open in 140 A.D.

11 The Beauty Kitchen

For natural-born scrubbers and slatherers

This kitchen has many recipes, but it is not a food outlet. It is all about nourishing the skin. Jo-Anne Chidley studied chemistry at university. She became a herbal botanist, and as a hobby made her own beauty products. Using her analytical skills, she discovered that many brands of cosmetics that claimed to be 'natural' were anything but. Spotting a gap in the market, she opened her own shop-cum-laboratory, making and selling products that are 100 per cent free from unnatural chemical ingredients.

Sourced from all over the world, components are many and varied – Abyssinian oil, heather and kelp to name but a few. Another is beeswax – Jo-Anne is a keen beekeeper. Ginger, coriander and cinnamon essential oils all have a culinary flavour, though not seahorse plankton, the microalgae that form the basis of one of the Beauty Kitchen's popular lines. Naturally, no seahorses are harmed in the process. Part of the proceeds goes to the Seahorse Trust, to aid in the preservation of these magical creatures.

With an ethos that is evangelical as well as entrepreneurial, the Beauty Kitchen enables customers to concoct their own products. Various DIY kits are on sale, including a can that looks as if it might contain soup but is for making lip balm. Workshops are held where participants are encouraged to create their own original creams and unguents. This involves fun, another ingredient that cannot be faked. They are popular with hen parties (but not, so far, with the 'stag' variety of prenuptial celebrations).

The Beauty Kitchen range is available at national chain Holland & Barrett, and online. But the small shop remains at the heart of the business. It is located in the historic Saltmarket, not one of the city's most stylish streets, but appropriate as it sells Himalayan salt – not for cooking, but for making soap or soothing weary limbs in a hot bath.

Address 117 Saltmarket, G1 5LF, +44 (0)141 552 9391, www.beautykitchen.co.uk |
Getting there Buses 2, 60, 60A, 61, 240, 255 to Watson Street | Hours Thu & Fri
11am–6.30pm, Sat 9.30am–5.30pm | Tip The Beauty Kitchen has attractive gift bags
in various tartans, made of ecologically sourced offcut material from a local kiltmaker.

12 The Berkeley Suite
From two-step to dubstep

The frontage declares these premises to be a pawnshop, with highest prices promised for Rolex watches, gold, silver and diamonds. But do not enter hoping for relief from penury. Inside is a late-night clubbing venue. The convincing façade is a gentle hoax and a clever piece of marketing, hinting that those who are not in the know should not be there anyway.

The second surprise is that, inside, the Berkeley is actually a bar and ballroom frozen in time. Chroniclers of Glasgow's social history have called it, proudly and ungrammatically, the 'dancingest city'. Scores of dance halls, many of them glittering mirrored palaces, once catered to the Glaswegian passion for quickstep, foxtrot, cha-cha and later jiving and the twist. A perfect night out for a young swain 'at the dancing' would end up with 'getting a lumber' – a potentially romantic journey based on the pretext of seeing a young lady safely home.

In an earlier life, the Berkeley Suite was a cut above the others, offering dinner to its smartly dressed clientele. The elegant Carrara marble staircase, chandeliers, tiling and mirrors remain in the largely untouched faded grandeur. The sprung dancefloor was already state of the art, and investment has gone into a cutting-edge sound system. The attire is now most likely to be torn jeans. The atmosphere in the basement ballroom can get hot and sweaty, but the upstairs bar is a calmer place for cocktails.

The music that makes the Berkeley Suite a must, as well as slightly musty, includes old-school disco, club-reggae, house and acid rock. You will be at home if you know what Walk n Skank might involve, or if you are familiar with the repertoires of the likes of Felix da Housecat, Richard Fearless from Death in Vegas, Optimo and Horse Meat Disco. Should you encounter the doors open during daylight, do not attempt to secure a cash advance on a personal item.

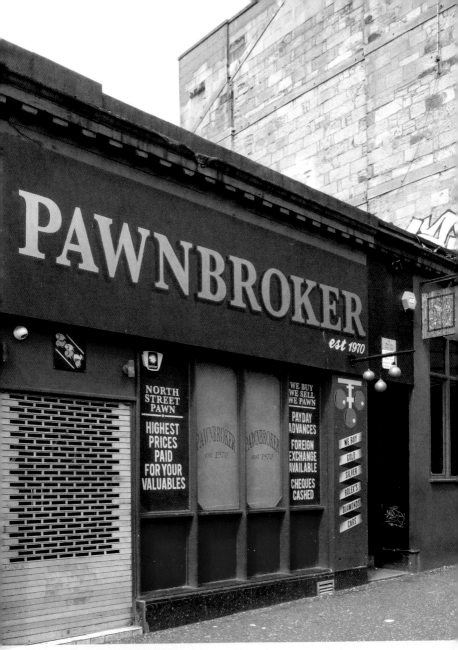

Address 237 North Street, G3 7DL, +44 (0)141 221 2451, www.berkeleysuite.com |
Getting there Buses 3, 17, 77, X76 to Granville Street | Hours Thu–Sat 10pm–3am |
Tip The premises next door at 239 North Street, also apparently pleading anonymity,
are home to Chinaski's, a bar and restaurant with a garden that is cool architecturally,
but often sunny in summertime.

13__The BFI Mediatheque

Keeping people in the picture

The BFI is the British Film Institute. A mediatheque is a library devoted to film and video. So what you have here is your own free cinema, where you can enjoy movies, TV programmes and documentaries selected from the BFI's extensive archives – the largest in the world.

The only BFI Mediatheque north of the border is housed in a handsomely restored building in Bridgeton, which began life in 1911 as the Olympia Theatre of Varieties. It has an authentic, dimly lit cinema ambience, with a cluster of comfortable, high-walled alcoves with banquette seating. Put on the headphones, select your film, and you are in your own private movie world. You can smuggle in a bag of sweeties, but definitely no hot dogs or drinks (and popcorn would be too messy).

Many of the over 2,000 titles currently on offer are not otherwise available online, due to copyright restrictions. The BFI has put together a special Scottish Reels selection: classic films include Hitchcock's 1939 spy adventure *The 39 Steps*, the original *Whisky Galore!* (1949), David Lean's *Madeleine* (a true-crime story set in Glasgow) and the cult *The Wicker Man*. Among the movies of local interest are Ken Loach's *My Name Is Joe*, Peter Mullan's *Orphans* and Bill Forsyth's *Gregory's Girl*. Landmark TV programmes include Peter Watkins' *Culloden*, a newsreel-style re-enactment of the battle, *Just Another Saturday*, Peter McDougall's earthy play about sectarian violence in Glasgow and *Rab C. Nesbitt*, Iain Pattison's comedy series about Govan Man. Sean Connery presents the documentary he directed about Glasgow shipbuilding, *The Bowler and the Bunnet*. You can also watch Connery conducting a personal tour around his home city of Edinburgh, which may save you a trip east to the capital. All this, plus a clip from 1954 of ballet-dancing coal miners, which is among a fascinating catalogue of mini-documentaries on life in Scotland.

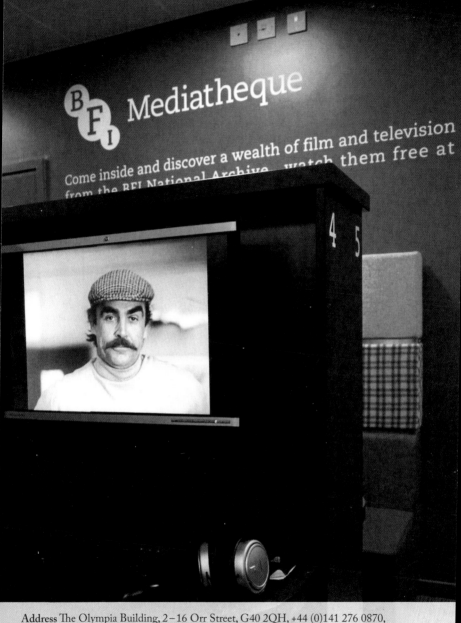

Address The Olympia Building, 2–16 Orr Street, G40 2QH, +44 (0)141 276 0870, www.glasgowlife.org.uk/libraries/your-local-library/bridgeton-library | **Getting there** Buses 18, 46, 64, 263, 765 to Anson Street; train to Bridgeton from Central Station | **Hours** Mon, Wed, Fri & Sat 10am–5pm, Tue & Thu 10am–8pm | **Tip** The Family Cakery is a *Magyar bolt* (Hungarian deli) stocking all kinds of Hungarian foods, and a place of pilgrimage for lovers of cakes and pastries (509 London Road, G40 1NQ, +44 (0)7933 554263).

14 Bike for Good

Cycling and recycling

Glasgow's thoroughfares are not overly blessed with safe cycle lanes, and some city drivers have not yet grasped the importance or courtesy of giving cyclists a wide berth. But the city is still a great place to pedal peacefully, along the variety of cycle paths that lead through parkland and along canal and riverbank. In most parts of Glasgow, the natives have stopped chucking spears at cycle convoys.

The first port of call should be Bike for Good, where you can pick up a free copy of their detailed map of Glasgow's cycling routes. This place is not just a shop; it is Scotland's largest bike recycling charity. As well as an emporium for bikes and accessories, it is an award-winning social enterprise, a collective where freewheeling philosophy is put into practice. Community programmes are in place to get people of all ages safely and cheaply out and about on bikes. Recycling is king. Old bikes are restored and sold at low prices. They are not second-hand; they are bespoke. DIY bike repair stations are available, with expert advice on hand.

Those interested in hiring a bike can do so via the computerised bike-sharing scheme Nextbike, which has a station outside. Bike for Good has human beings who will get you on your way and give advice on places to go. Serious cyclists may choose to go all the way to Loch Lomond, or even further afield to Aberfoyle, for a touch of the Trossachs – not a medical condition from too much cycling, but a magical tour of the lochs and glens north of the city in Rob Roy country. A 27-mile canalside route will take you through central Scotland to the Falkirk Wheel, a unique rotating boat lift, and on to see the impressive *Kelpies* – 30-metre-tall sculptures of horse's heads. These long-distance adventures are for the hardened enthusiast. Others will prefer less challenging spins within the city, such as the 6-mile traffic-free Glasgow Waterways Loop. Ask at Bike for Good about organised social rides.

Address 65 Haugh Road, G3 8TX, +44 (0)141 248 5409, www.bikeforgood.org.uk |
Getting there Buses 2, 100 to Haugh Road | Hours Mon – Sat 9am – 5pm (Wed
until 8pm) | Tip Nearby at 1223 Argyle Street is the Argyle Tree, the oldest and for a
long time the only tree on the long thoroughfare that runs through the centre of the
city. The story is that the tree was grown by mistake, its seed being in a clump of earth
containing primrose roots, transplanted some 160 years ago into the front garden of
the tenement building. The aged ash now towers high above the rooftops.

15__ The Bon Accord

Nip in for a dram

As the song goes, 'Show me the way to the next whisky bar...' Glasgow is not short of premises specialising in Scotland's national drink. The Bon Accord is a family-run pub that has regularly been named UK Whisky Bar of the Year. Its selection of 400 single malt whiskies is not the biggest in town but as owner Paul McDonagh says, 'We don't go for quantity. We seek out the rare and the old.' Like the 70-year-old Glenlivet – the most expensive at £900 a nip.

Malt whisky aficionados come from all over the world to sample the gems in the Bon Accord collection. Scotland's more exclusive malts can fetch thousands of pounds per bottle at auction, and customers here are unfazed by hefty bills after their long voyages of discovery. The well-informed staff are on hand to discuss the intricate details of varieties from the Highlands, Islands and Lowlands. Or perhaps a smooth Japanese Hibiki. 'Our visitors are serious and knowledgeable,' says Paul. Those who are not hard-core connoisseurs or winners of the Euromillions lottery may opt for the malt of the month at around £3.

The language used in tasting notes for malt whisky can be as elaborate, and perhaps as pretentious, as the terminology for Bordeaux clarets. A whisky may have a fascinating nose of polished grand piano, exotic fruits, Haribos and scented tea. Or treacle sponge, vanilla custard, garam masala and antique cigar box. You are unlikely to hear such terms at the Bon Accord. It is a place of pilgrimage for lovers of *uisge-beatha* (water of life, i.e. whisky) but mainly it is a hospitable Glasgow bar. It is also known for its wide range of ales, with about 1,000 on offer over the year, on a rotating basis. You may be tempted by the local tradition of a 'hauf an' hauf' – a half-pint of beer accompanied by a spirit. Whatever your tipple, line your stomach with a plate of home-made steak pie from the pub grub menu.

Address 153 North Street, G3 7DA, +44 (0)141 248 4427, www.bonaccordpub.com |
Getting there Buses 3, 17, 77, X76 to Granville Street or bus 2 to St Vincent Terrace;
train to Charing Cross | Hours Mon–Sat 11am–midnight, Sun 12.30pm–midnight |
Tip On your way home, take a look at the Cameron fountain at nearby Charing Cross.
It's not just the effects of the whisky you may have had. This Doulton terracotta
drinking fountain, a tribute to a Glasgow MP, really is leaning seriously to one side,
tower-of-Pisa style.

16 Braehead Curling

Have a go at the roaring game

About 500 years ago the Scots invented the winter sport of curling, which involves propelling really heavy lumps of stone across an icy surface. This was shortly after Scotland had given birth to golf, a pursuit where players use a stick to chase a ball over uneven terrain to a small distant hole in the ground. Then there is tossing the caber – throwing tree trunks into the air. Let's just say that the Scots are good at strange games.

The earliest definitive curling stone dates from 1511. The first report of a match, involving monks at Paisley Abbey, was written in 1541. Stones can weigh nearly 20 kilos, but brute force is not involved. It's about measured propulsion and the precise calculation of a curved trajectory. Vigorous brushing of the ice is required to control the speed and degree of curl. Curling is known as the roaring game, from the sound created by the glide of the smooth granite stones. It has been nicknamed 'chess on ice', as an important aspect of play is the removal of opposing teams' stones from the target area of concentric circles.

The sport has been played at more than 2,500 locations across Scotland, with many towns and villages having curling ponds. A bonspiel, or grand match, took place when a suitable lake froze over sufficiently for thousands of curlers to congregate, compete and have a social sip of whisky. But Scotland no longer has cold enough winters, and there has not been a bonspiel for nearly 40 years.

Curling is still hugely popular but is now played mainly indoors. The ice rink at Braehead is a modern venue where players of all ages hone their skills, and newcomers can have their first taste of this cool sport, with coaching on hand. Curling is a Winter Olympics sport in which Scottish teams still win gold medals, albeit under the flag of Team GB. Eve Muirhead, who coaches at Braehead, is one of the world's leading players.

Address intu Braehead, King's Inch Road, G51 4BN, +44 (0)141 885 4611, www.curlbraehead.co.uk | **Getting there** Buses 901, 906, 907, X7, X23 to intu Braehead | **Hours** Check website for dates and times of Curling Sweep events for beginners | **Tip** The intu Braehead leisure centre also has a ski and snowboard slope, an ice climb wall and a Baltic ice bar; wrap up warm to have a cocktail.

17 — Britannia Panopticon

Memories of music-hall mayhem

In Victorian times, Glasgow's teeming working classes sought diversion from their dismal daily existence in boozy, bawdy, smoky, disorderly music halls. Shows regularly descended into mayhem, as the packed audience attempted to inflict bodily injury on performers they didn't like. They felt that the penny entrance fee gave them the right to hurl not only abuse but also objects at them, from rotten vegetables to pieces of metal purloined from factory and shipyard.

Opened in 1857, the Britannia in Glasgow's Trongate is the world's oldest surviving music hall. In 1906, it was transformed into the Britannia Panopticon by the showman A. E. Pickard, who incorporated a zoo, freak show, fairground and waxworks into the building. One of his many stunts was to have Solomon, a chimpanzee, dress up in top hat and tails and undergo a 'wedding ceremony' with his mate Betsy, also in bridal attire. On another occasion, the shameless Pickard arranged for Solomon to be arrested as drunk and disorderly by the police.

The Panopticon continued to be a leading music hall, hosting such stars as Sir Harry Lauder, as well as the first stage performance by a 16-year-old Glasgow resident called Stan Laurel, later to become a world-famous film star with his comedy partner Oliver Hardy. But in 1938 it went the way of all music halls and closed its doors, in the face of competition from the cinema.

In 1997, Judith Bowers visited the boarded-up theatre, fell in love with the place, and made it her mission to save it. With the co-operation of the building's owners and the help of a group of dedicated volunteers, she reopened the hall and set up a trust to give it a future. Though very much a work in progress, it now hosts a range of events, including variety performances. Just as in the days of the music hall's legendary dancing girls, the Britannia is once more alive and kicking.

Address 1st floor, 117 Trongate, G1 5HD, +44 (0)141 553 0840, www.britanniapanopticon.org | **Getting there** Buses 2, 60, 60A, 61, 64, 240 to Candleriggs; subway to St Enoch; entrance in lane beside Mitchell's Amusement Arcade | **Hours** Tue–Sat noon–5pm; check website for details of evening events | **Tip** Round the corner, Café Cossachok offers a taste of Russia and other parts of the former Soviet Union – blinis, borscht and other goodies just like your babushka used to make, plus authentic vodkas, great cocktails and reasonably priced wines (10 King Street, G1 5Q, +44 (0)141 553 0733).

18 Bud Neill Memorial

The world's only two-legged equestrian statue

This monument was erected in 1992 in homage to cartoonist, poet, surrealist and philosopher Bud Neill. Growing up in the west of Scotland in the 1920s and 1930s, Bud spent too many hours in local cinemas watching cowboy movies. These became the inspiration for his most famous cartoon strip, which first appeared in 1949 in the *Evening Times*. He set it in the imaginary Glasgow township of Calton Creek, which just happened to be in the Wild West of Arizona. The main three characters feature in the statue: Lobey Dosser, the diminutive sheriff, his arch enemy, Rank Bajin, and El Fideldo (Elfie for short), the wee horse. Bud Neill said that Elfie was a biped because he wasn't any good at drawing horses with four legs. The statue is small in a typically Glaswegian way, but it would have been a lot smaller if it had been made life size, 8 centimetres being the height of the cartoon strip frame.

Apart from some visiting Native Americans, Calton Creek (named after a district in Glasgow's East End) was populated by Glaswegian folk, who spoke and behaved as if they were in Scotland. Big Chief Toffy Teeth and his tribe were treated with courtesy, and offered fish and chips. The cartoon strip was a huge success, with queues outside newsagents of people eager to read that day's episode. But it was only a fraction of Bud Neill's output of hilarious and forensic wit about Glasgow life and culture.

The statue was paid for by public subscription, most of the donations coming from honorary deputy sheriffs of Calton Creek with fond memories of his humour. It has suffered from its own popularity, with too many people (including inebriated adults from nearby pubs) mounting the already overburdened horse. El Fideldo has now had three operations to repair broken legs, the last being major surgery to allow children to have a photo opportunity aboard the wee horse.

Address Woodlands Road, at the corner of Woodlands Gate, G3 6LF | Getting there Buses 4, 4A, 15, X25A, X77 to Woodlands Gate | Tip The Arlington Bar at 130 Woodlands Road houses what is claimed to be the original Stone of Destiny, on which early Scottish kings were crowned. The stone was taken to Westminster Abbey in 1296, after Scotland was invaded by England. In 1950 it was returned to Scotland by radical students. The story goes that the stone later recovered by the authorities (and now in Edinburgh Castle) was a copy, and that the real one is in the Arlington. After a few pints, you may be convinced of this.

19 Buffalo Bill Statue

The sad story of Kicking Bear

You might wonder what Buffalo Bill (aka William Cody), is doing in a little park in Dennistoun, sitting astride a bucking bronco. Cody was a US army scout during the 'Indian Wars'. He earned his nickname by slaughtering thousands of buffalo for the US army, killing off one or two Native Americans on the way, and later became famous for his Buffalo Bill Wild West show, which came to the East End of Glasgow in 1891 and played to packed houses for three months.

Among the Native Americans with a bit part in the Buffalo Bill show was a Lakota chief called Kicking Bear. He was no 'stage injun' (as Native Americans were called then) – he'd fought at the Little Big Horn, and was active with his uncle Sitting Bull in the Ghost Dance movement, which promoted the resurgence of the Native American tribes and the defeat of the US army.

Shortly after the shameful day when 279 men, women and children from his tribe were murdered at the Battle of Wounded Knee, Kicking Bear was arrested for his resistance activities. He was given the choice of jail or leaving his homeland to join Buffalo Bill's show. Kicking Bear ended up in Dennistoun, suffering the indignity of performing his tribal dances in a circus setting. There was further humiliation when the show's manager sold a collection of 'Indian relics', including a Ghost Shirt from Wounded Knee, to Glasgow's Kelvingrove Museum. We do not know how Kicking Bear reacted to this. But his colleague Charging Thunder lived up to his name by attacking the show manager with a lump of wood. Despite a plea in mitigation that his glass of lemonade had been spiked with whisky in a Dennistoun pub, Charging Thunder was sentenced to 30 days in Barlinnie Prison.

At the end of his stint with Buffalo Bill, Kicking Bear was put on a ship back to the USA. When it docked in New York, he was arrested on board and taken back to prison.

Address Whitehill Street, G31 2LR, at the corner of Finlay Drive | Getting there Buses 8, 41, 46, 60, 60A, 90 to Bathgate Street; train to Duke Street | Hours Unrestricted | Tip Dennistoun Bar-B-Que is nearby if you want to continue the Wild West theme and risk it for a brisket, fast-food style (585 Duke Street, G31 1PY).

20___The Byres Road Lanes
A warren of alternative trading places

Glasgow has the best shopping in the UK outside London, with the city centre 'Style Mile' hosting the biggest names and brands in world fashion. For a more original odyssey, the cobbled lanes of the West End offer an alternative retail experience. Clustered around Hillhead Subway station on Byres Road, a network of lanes that once housed run-down workshops and garages is now a bohemian destination, with a colourful range of shops, galleries, pubs, restaurants and beer gardens as well as a two-screen boutique cinema.

From the Subway station, cross Byres Road and wander down Dowanside Lane, home to a range of independent traders specialising in vintage fashion and accessories, jewellery, artisanal homeware, records, books and comics. Don't miss the aptly named Relic, where there is something for everyone – if you can find it, lurking under the mountains of bric-a-brac. Continue to Ruthven Mews Arcade, where 11 shops offer more upmarket but affordable antiques and collectibles. Keep your eyes peeled for signs indicating poster shops, yoga lofts, beauty salons and interior design studios.

Back across Byres Road, and first left from the rising hill of Great George Street, follow Creswell Lane to climb back in time at the retrocentric two-storey De Courcy's Arcade, plunge into a dungeon of design at the Nancy Smillie Shop and Gallery, or have a wizard time in the Harry Potter store.

About turn and head for Ashton Lane, where a jaunty 3-D gable end decoration announces that it's Guinness time. In 1976 Ronnie Clydesdale brought this lane back to life when he moved his pioneering restaurant, the Ubiquitous Chip, into an old undertaker's stable, launching a new wave of Scottish cookery that championed local and seasonal produce. In an ironic comment on long-standing perceptions of Caledonian cuisine, Ronnie ordained that not a single potato would be deep-fried there.

Address Start at Dowanside Lane, G12 9BZ | Getting there Buses 8, 8A, 90, 372 to Roxburgh Street; subway to Hillhead | Tip The Stand Comedy Club, 333 Woodlands Road, G3 6NG, offers nightly stand-up humour, with a mix of local and visiting performers (7.30pm−1am, shows start at 8.30pm; +44 (0)141 212 3389).

21 — Caledonia Road Church

Gem that got lost in traffic

It is Glasgow's most elegant ruin. What is left of the Caledonia Road United Presbyterian Church serves as a memorial to Alexander 'Greek' Thomson, the eminent and prolific architect of the Victorian era. With its impressive Italianate tower and Greek temple frontage, it is certainly a more fitting reminder of his life than his monument in the nearby Southern Necropolis. Thomson died in 1875, and was buried in a lair beside 5 of his 12 children, who had perished in a cholera epidemic. Over the years, the huge graveyard became subject to severe neglect. Thomson's headstone was damaged, and in the 1950s it disappeared. The great architect lay uncommemorated. Then in 2000, after a resurgence of interest in his work, a new monument was erected at the grave. It is a large lump of black granite bearing the single word 'Thomson', which scarcely does justice to the man.

Thomson became well known for incorporating elements of Greek, Egyptian and other classical and oriental styles into his work. In the middle of the 19th century he filled Glasgow and its environs with villas of all sizes, a castle or two, terraced houses and commercial premises. He also designed what have been described as three of the finest Romantic Classical churches in the world – all three of them in the city.

The Caledonia Road Church was the first; he was also a member of its congregation. By the 1960s it lay empty, and in 1965 it was largely destroyed by fire. Its remains are now isolated on a traffic island. Various ambitious plans to revive the ruin, the last historic building in Gorbals, have come to nothing, though local activists have taken over the land inside the derelict church to use as a garden and space for events. The preferred local plan is to build inside its shell, and redevelop Thomson's iconic church as a location symbolising the new Gorbals.

Address 1 Caledonia Road, G5 9DP | Getting there Buses 21, 31, 75, 267, 314, 324 to Cumberland Street | Hours Viewable from the outside only | Tip The last Alexander Thomson church still functioning is the Glasgow City Free Church in St Vincent Street, stunning both inside and out. The best way to see it is to attend a service there (www.glasgowcityfreechurch.org).

22 The Carbeth Huts

Social housing in the forest

In Gaelic it is *bothan beinne*; in Scots, but an' ben. In English, more prosaically, the word is hut. In whatever language, you don't have to be a wealthy Glaswegian to have a wee house in the country. Proof of this equality of rural opportunity is to found at Carbeth Hill, just 10 miles from the city, where 150 cabins nestle in a spectacular woodland setting. The residents are known as the Carbeth Hutters. Their story began in 1918 when the landowner granted camping rights to soldiers recovering from the traumas of war, to enjoy a spot of rest and recuperation. Permanent structures were built over the years. The huts had to be small, in natural wood or painted green to blend into the landscape.

In the 1920s and 1930s, more and more people were seeking fresh-air respite from polluted towns and cities, and the community grew. For decades, a campfire at nearby Craigallian Loch burnt perma-nently as a sign of welcome. At weekends and summer holidays, Carbeth became a hive of country pursuits – cycling, hillwalking, rock climbing and swimming, in a pool created by damming a stream. Some hutters had already exercised vigorously by walking most of the 10 miles to the site. Those from Clydebank would trek across the Kilpatrick Hills. Most importantly, Carbeth was a place where city children could thrive. A sign today advises motorists: 'Watch your speed! Free range children.'

In 2013, after years of conflict and intense negotiations with the landowners, the hutters managed an amicable deal to buy the 90-acre site for £1.75 million. After some long overdue land reform, it is now easier to build a small dwelling in a rural environment in Scotland, and a hutting revival is going on. Visitors are welcome to look around the social revolution that is Carbeth, where there is an ongoing programme of upgrading existing huts, and sensitive building on new forest sites.

Address Stockiemuir Road, G63 9AY, www.carbethhutters.co.uk | Getting there By car: head north on A809, turn right on B821, 400 metres after Carbeth Inn; bus C8 from Buchanan Bus Station (Mon–Sat, limited service, morning and early evening only) | Tip It is possible to become a Carbeth hut owner, but the waiting list is long, and new members are expected to make a firm commitment to the ethos and aims of the community.

23 Cartha Rugby Club

A game, a pie and a pint

If you have never been to a rugby match, Glasgow is a good place to give it a try. The city's professional team, Glasgow Warriors, competes at the highest level in Europe. Their Friday night matches are usually tense and exciting. Another way to sample rugby as it has been played in Scotland for nearly 150 years is to visit one of Glasgow's amateur clubs. The Cartha Queen's Park ground is in a beautiful parkland setting, there is a decent quality of play, and it is a most sociable place to visit. From its foundation in 1889, the club based near the River Cart (the origin of its name) has been a hive of diverse sporting endeavour. As well as the oval and round ball versions of football, members of what was then known as Cartha Athletic Club used to play cricket, tennis, hockey, cycling, croquet and ping-pong. Activities also included dances, drama and opera. Nowadays the sport is rugby.

Watching rugby action at close quarters, the uninitiated may conclude that in the midst of some ferocious unarmed combat, a game involving an oval ball has broken out. The rules of rugby football will be a mystery to beginners, especially when the players have piled into a heap on top of the ball. Fortunately, there is usually a learned spectator on hand to explain why the referee has awarded one of the teams a free kick – as well as many others to disagree on the intricacies of the rulebook.

When the game is over, players from both sides and spectators gather in the clubhouse for a drink or two and some food, usually involving Scotch pies. There may be singing, though possibly not of operatic quality. Rugby songs have traditionally been crude and sexist. But club rugby has changed; women are no longer there just to make the sandwiches, but are playing the game in increasing numbers. Cartha has five women's teams, who may even have some feminist songs about men.

Address 92 Dumbreck Road, G41 4SN, +44 (0)141 427 1593, www.carthaqp.co.uk | Getting there Train to Dumbreck from Central Station (Paisley Canal line), then 12-minute walk; turn right across motorway bridge, then right again on to signposted footpath to Pollok Park | Hours Sept–Apr, check website for dates, times and details of fixtures | Tip Cartha is home each May to the annual Glasgow City Sevens tournament. Rugby Sevens is a variant of the game with teams of 7 players instead of the usual 15.

24_ The Cathedral Lamp Posts

The bird, the bell, the fish and the tree

Glasgow never misses an opportunity to show off its coat of arms. It is to be seen in all its glory not only on the cover of this book but on bridges, benches, T-shirts, tattoos, teacups and, in a deconstructed form, on the lovely lamp posts outside the cathedral. It tells the story of St Mungo, founder of the city – a sixth-century tale of fantasy, exaggeration, sex and violence in a dysfunctional family. Typical Glasgow, you might say, except that it seems Mungo was a Welsh-speaking lad of vaguely royal descent, born in the east of Scotland, whose mother was raped and made pregnant by some Welsh warrior. Her father reacted by throwing her off a steep hill, then setting her adrift in a small boat. She survived and her son was born. To complicate matters, he was originally named Kentigern.

This is all before we get to the detail of the bird, the bell, the fish and the tree on the coat of arms. After his turbulent birth, Kentigern was adopted into a Christian community and trained to be a missionary. As a youth he performed miracles, bringing a robin back to life (the bird), making a hazel branch burst into flames by the power of prayer (the tree) and covering up a royal lady's allegedly adulterous behaviour, with some trickery involving a ring and a salmon (the fish). Mungo's life is not so much a coat of arms as a script for a box set on Netflix, especially since it is believed by some that he had dealings with Merlin, the wizard of King Arthur and the Round Table fame.

Mungo brought his Christian zeal west and set up his church in a small green place, where his cathedral and city now flourish. He converted local pagans with his piety and preaching – and probably some coercion and conflict, which remains in Glasgow's religious DNA to this day.

Address Cathedral Square, G4 0XA | Getting there Buses 19, 19A, 38, 38B, 38C, 38E, 57, 57A to Glebe Street | Tip At the west end of the Cathedral precinct, stop and say hello to the impressive statue of David Livingstone, the Scottish missionary. He was famous for his religious and medical work in Africa, for trying to find the source of the Nile, for getting lost and for being found, with the greeting 'Doctor Livingstone, I presume.'

25 Central Gurdwara

Meet the lions and princesses

The 15,000 or so Sikhs resident in Scotland make up just 0.2 per cent of the population, yet their new temple in Glasgow is the largest place of worship of any faith in the whole country. It was built big because the Sikhs are expecting a lot of guests. The gurdwara is open to visitors of all colours, creeds, races and religions. It is a place for prayer and learning, but also for healing the sick, feeding the hungry and providing rest for the weary traveller. Thus a doctor is usually available during services, the *langar* (kitchen) is open every day, offering a simple vegetarian meal free of charge, and there is restful space for contemplation of whatever god the visitor may believe in.

The Sikh religion may appear complicated, with its 10 gurus (spiritual leaders) and their histories. There are 1,430 pages of holy scripture, on occasions both sad and happy, which are read aloud in their entirety in services that can last for up to 48 hours. But the three pillars of Sikh wisdom are simple, and they are explained to visitors via the teachings on the gurdwara walls. One of the pillars is that of generosity and sharing. Another is to work diligently and honestly. The first pillar is daily prayer and meditation. Male Sikhs all have the name Singh (lion), and females Kaur (princess).

The gurdwara's glistening gold dome has changed the Glasgow skyline. The massive three-storey building, in pink stone imported from Rajasthan, seems to glitter itself even on a grey day. It was opened in 2016 after a six-year construction programme, the fruit of 20 years of planning, thrifty fund-raising of £8 million and much hands-on labour by the community. The Sikhs first came to Scotland more than a century ago, when a maharajah settled in Perthshire. Most of their subsequent immigration has been to Glasgow, where they have won a reputation for industry and innovation. The turban and the kilt are often to be seen together.

Address 138 Berkeley Street, G3 7HY, +44 (0)141 221 6698, www.central-gurdwara.com | Getting there Buses 3, 17, 77, X76 to Elderslie Street | Hours Daily 7am–8pm | Tip Housed in a lovely former tearoom, Mother India restaurant lives up to its name as a cradle of authentic curry cuisine, whilst being very Glaswegian (28 Westminster Terrace, G3 7RU, +44 (0)141 221 1663).

26__ Central Station
Locomotives and lost platforms

There is an old story of a country lad who took a train trip to see Glasgow. When he returned to his village, he told a tale of a marvellous big city that was all under glass. He'd got no further than Central Station. Its roof extends for two square miles, contains 48,000 panes of glass, and is said to be the biggest of its kind in the world. With its attached hotel, the station really is a fascinating city within a city. Its impressive gates were recently repainted glorious green and gold. They had formerly been black, it is said, out of respect for Prince Albert, late consort of Queen Victoria. Strange, since Albert died in 1862 and the station was not built until 1879. But Victoria did take her mourning seriously.

The gates should really have been painted black in mourning for the village of Grahamston, once a thriving commercial centre for Glasgow's trade in tobacco, rum, sugar, cotton, coffee, timber, animal hides and grain, that was largely demolished in the 1870s to make way for the station. A complete history of the station is provided on the tours of the spacious concourse and cavernous basement conducted by railway worker Paul Lyons. He is a marvellous raconteur, whose stories place it at the heart of Glasgow's social history. There is pathos in the disused platform in the bowels of the station that served as a mortuary for Scottish soldiers who fell in World War I. There is humour as Paul tells of the 40,000 who turned out to welcome comedy film duo Laurel and Hardy, and specifically the Glaswegian who shook Hardy warmly by the hand and stole his gold watch in the process. The visits of singing cowboy Roy Rogers, who had an unfortunate experience with whisky, and of a young John F. Kennedy also feature.

The ebb and flow of the busy station can best be savoured from the windows of Champagne Central, a striking oval-shaped watering hole in the Grand Central Hotel that overlooks the concourse.

Address Gordon Street, G1 3SL | **Getting there** Buses 4, 4A, 6, 7, 7A, 21, 75, 263, 267, 309 and others to Central Station; train (obviously) from stations throughout the city | **Hours** Tours: 10am–4pm, dates and times vary, see www.glasgowcentraltours.co.uk; Champagne Central: Mon–Sat 9am–late, Sun noon–late | **Tip** The Arches, a former theatre and clubbing venue in a warren of cellars below Central Station, has been given a new lease of life as a weekend street-food emporium (253 Argyle Street, G2 8DL, Fri & Sat 11am–10pm).

27 The Centre for Scottish Culture

Step gaily in a historic setting

No visit to Glasgow is complete without a night of traditional Scottish ceilidh dancing. (Pronounced 'kaylee', this is the Gaelic word for 'party'.) The fast and furious Strip the Willow involves a row of at least four couples taking turns to link arms, spin madly and hurl their partners at other dancers. The Dashing White Sergeant is vigorous but not so wild. The Gay Gordons is calm and elegant by comparison.

A great place to dip your toes into ceilidh dancing is at one of the weekly classes, with a live band, held in the fabulous Georgian church that is now a centre for Scottish music, song and dance. St Andrew's in the Square opened in 1756 as the parish church for Glasgow's wealthy tobacco barons. The design was closely based on London's St Martin-in-the-Fields. The merchants praised the Lord in an egregiously splendid setting, funded by fortunes gathered from usurious manipulation of planters in the American colonies and the shameful trade in slaves from West Africa. Glasgow's Presbyterians were in a race to build the city's first post-Reformation church against the Episcopalians, who were busy erecting their St Andrew's by the Green further down the same street.

The parishioners eventually abandoned their church as moneyed Glaswegians migrated to the west of the city in the 19th century. St Andrew's and its handsome square became isolated in slum territory. The last service was held in 1993, and its future was in doubt. Then the Glasgow Building Preservation Trust stepped in to save the church and restore the adjacent Georgian houses in what is now Glasgow's most beautiful and peaceful square. The interior of the church has been stripped of its Victorian additions and is a stylish setting for concerts, weddings and, of course, ceilidhs.

Address 1 St Andrew's Square, G1 5PP, +44 (0)141 559 5902,
www.standrewsinthesquare.com | Getting there Buses 2, 18, 60, 60A, 61, 64, 240,
255, 263 to Watson Street | Hours Guided tours: Feb–Nov, Tue 11am–1.30pm;
Ceilidh dance classes: Wed 7.15pm; phone +44 (0)1324 716855 for details | Tip
The church basement has been turned into Café Source to complement its new use.
Among its Scottish dishes is a tasty Cullen skink traditional fish soup
(+44 (0)141 548 6020, www.cafesource.co.uk).

28 __ The Climbing Centre

Heavenly pursuits

Glasgow has a reputation for unpretentious friendliness, where the self-important are given short shrift. But there is one place in the city that social climbers are welcomed with open arms. A former church in the Ibrox area is home to the Glasgow Climbing Centre, where you can both scale dizzy heights and make new friends.

Reaching up to the ornate exposed beams in the two-storey nave of this sturdy 150-year-old building are 16-metre walls that offer challenges for climbers of all abilities, and all ages from seven up. There is a mix of vertical and overhanging routes. There are autobelay set-ups for solo ascents, and options for those able to buddy-up and rope with another climber. Do not worry about the technicalities, as introductory sessions are available for the inexperienced. Even seasoned scalers must pass a quick assessment before they can get to grips with the walls. All necessary equipment can be hired at the centre. Downstairs there is a well-equipped bouldering room, where you can tackle short 'problems' at a low level without ropes, with the comfort of a thick mat to crash on to if you fall. At the other extreme is the opportunity, weather permitting, to abseil down the outside of the high pointed steeple – one great bonus of turning a church into a mountain.

After some energetic indoor mountaineering, head up the spiral staircase to the Balcony Café and enjoy a well-earned reward on high, bathed in the dappled multi-coloured light cast by the large stained-glass window. A range of international dishes is available, as well as artisan coffee and cake.

The building, in a mixture of Gothic and Early English styles, opened in 1868 as the Ibrox United Presbyterian Church. After an ecumenical merger in 1900, it became the United Free Church. From 1978 it was a Methodist church, until the early 1990s and its conversion into the Climbing Centre.

Address 534 Paisley Road West, G51 1RN, +44 (0)141 427 9550, www.glasgowclimbingcentre.com | Getting there Buses 9, 9A, 10, 38, 38A, 153 to Paisley Road West; subway to Cessnock, then 10-minute walk | Hours Mon–Fri 11am–10pm, Sat & Sun 9am–6pm | Tip The Climbing Centre is only a few hundred metres from Ibrox Stadium, home of the world-famous Rangers Football Club. Public transport will be busy before and after the home games of the 'Teddy Bears'.

29 __ The Clydeport Building
When Glasgow ruled the waves

Hemmed in by modern office blocks on the street called Broomielaw, the grand former headquarters of the Clyde Navigation Trust are a reminder of the days when Glasgow was one of the busiest ports in the world. The first Broomielaw quay was built in 1688, and as Glasgow's status as a trading city grew the wharves bustled with ships offloading tobacco, cotton, sugar, grain and other profitable resources from far-off lands. The other import at the Broomielaw was people. It was the landing point for the hundreds of thousands of immigrants who came to the city with a mixture of desperation and hope, fleeing hunger and repression. There was also a considerable human export, in the boatloads of Scottish soldiers sent to fight and die in Britain's imperial wars. Scotland's anti-colonialist anthem, *Freedom Come All Ye*, remembers the fatherless 'weans frae pit heid and clachan' (children from mining communities and Highland villages) who 'mourn the ships sailing doon the Broomielaw'.

The Clyde Navigation Trust was in charge of all the traffic on the river, and the building reflected its role as an important and wealthy city institution. From the ships' prows emerging from the walls to the over-the-top statuary on the roof, an unmistakable statement is made about Glasgow's connections with the sea. Poseidon and Amphitrite, Greek god and goddess of the sea, are both depicted clutching tridents and surrounded by seahorses. Demeter, goddess of corn and harvests, represents Glasgow's former role as a major importer of grain from the American prairies.

The building's interior is suitably opulent, particularly the domed meeting hall, but it is still a place of business and is seldom open for visitors. A peek into the fabulous tiled entrance hall is worthwhile. Outside, just look up and absorb the history of a building that shames Glasgow's unsuccessful efforts to cherish its waterfront heritage by preserving more of Broomielaw's seafaring ambience.

Address 16 Robertson Street, G2 8DS | Getting there Short walk from Central Station; subway to St Enoch | Hours Viewable from the outside only | Tip Clyde Cruises offer a variety of boat trips from Yorkhill Quay, including a three-hour round voyage down the river to Dumbarton Rock (May–Oct, +44 (0)1475 721282, www.clydecruises.com).

30___Cottonrake Bakery
Join the patisserie revolution

There has been a renaissance of the craft of baking in Glasgow. It has become fashionable to refer to this movement as artisan, and many of the craftspeople who have set up in competition with purveyors of mass-produced fare from industrial premises are, indeed, artists. Glaswegians, who have long had a taste for baked goods, sweet and savoury, have taken kindly to this new wave retailing quality, handcrafted delicacies.

The Cottonrake is a perfect example of the genre. And it has an extra ingredient: a sense of humour. The neon sign in the window, the work of local artist and Turner Prize nominee David Shrigley, advertises 'Donut Repair'. Inside the bustling and usually crowded premises, once a sadly neglected outlet of a big bakery chain, there is serious eating going on. Breakfast choices range from croissants, *pain au chocolat* and toasted sourdough bread to the traditional Scottish roll with many fillings. The bacon roll comes with green leaves and actually is rocket science.

The Cottonrake sausage roll (not to be confused with the roll on sausage) is a substantial flaky pastry concoction of pork shoulder and black pudding. Some customers take them home to smother in baked beans. One regular adds slightly caramelised scallops, which elevates his takeaway dish to Michelin-star level.

For elevenses, or at any other time of day, there are the scones and cakes. The meringues and white chocolate tarts are particularly toothsome. Ingredients are seasonal, lavish fruitfulness in summer and mellow nuttiness in winter. Customers on a diet can satisfy themselves with a fine cup of coffee and get a vicarious bakery buzz just from watching the artisans at work. Ironically (and Glasgow is a great city for irony) one item you will not find on the Cottonrake menu is the doughnut, broken or otherwise. Despite the neon sign, their kitchen is not in fact equipped with a deep fryer.

Address 497 Great Western Road, G12 8HL, +44 (0)7910 282040, www.cottonrake.com |
Getting there Buses 6, 6A, 10A to Hamilton Park Avenue; subway to Kelvinbridge |
Hours Daily 8am–6pm | **Tip** For artisan doughnuts visit Tantrum Doughnuts at 27 Old
Dumbarton Road, G3 8RD, where skilled pastry chefs make their small-batch delicacies
daily. When they're gone, they're gone. Adventurous flavours include pistachio and
hisbiscus, maple candied bacon and crème brulée (Tue–Fri 9am–6pm, Sat 10am–6pm,
Sun 10am–5pm, +44 (0)141 339 9319).

31 Crookston Castle

Ruined by a cannon called Meg

Glasgow's only surviving medieval castle stands in the middle of a vast estate – not the policies of some duke or earl, but a social housing estate, or 'scheme'. It was an Anglo-Norman knight called Sir Robert de Croc, given land by the Scottish king, who put the Croc into Crookston about the year 1170. He built an earth and timber fortification on the hill where the castle now stands. The land subsequently came into the hands of the Stewarts, who had become increasingly powerful after fighting alongside Robert the Bruce in the ultimately successful wars of Scottish independence. The family prospered, gathering noble titles in Scotland and in France, where they led armies for the French kings. Around 1400, the Darnley Stewarts transformed Crookston into a substantial stone castle. But they picked the wrong side in an internecine conflict between the Stewart kings, and in 1489 the castle came under siege and was largely destroyed, courtesy of Mons Meg, Scotland's biggest ever cannon. It was patched up but left in a reduced state.

Crookston's next major role in Scottish history was as the place in 1574 where Mary, Queen of Scots became betrothed to Henry Stewart, Lord Darnley. History was not kind to Mary or Darnley, but their son, James VI of Scotland and I of England, was the first of the line of Stewart monarchs of Great Britain.

The castle went through a series of owners before eventually being abandoned. It became a playground for children from the Pollok scheme, but it remains a place redolent of history, now looked after by Historic Environment Scotland, and still free to visit. The impressive barrel vault and the one tower that survived Mons Meg give imaginative visitors a feeling of what once went on within these walls. A certain amount of agility is required to climb the tower, negotiating medieval staircases and more modern ladders for a wonderful view over southern Glasgow.

Address Off Brockburn Road, G53 5RY, +44 (0)141 883 9606, www.historicenvironment.scot | **Getting there** Bus 3 to Silverburn Bus Station, then 49 to top of Brockburn Road or 15-minute walk; train to Crookston from Central Station (Paisley Canal line), then 20-minute walk; follow the path from Brockburn Road up the hill to the castle | **Hours** Apr–Sept, daily 9.30am–5.30pm; Oct–Mar, Sat–Wed 10am–4pm | **Tip** Since you have come all this way, the nearby Silverburn Centre on Barrhead Road is not the worst place in the city to shop.

32 Cuningar Loop
How grunge turned into green

This is the tale of two areas of blight in the East End of the city that came together to make a woodland park. The Cuningar Loop, where the River Clyde takes a U-shaped meander, was for 50 years from 1810 home to the reservoirs that provided Glasgow with its drinking water. After a vast new system was constructed to supply the city with sparkling healthy water from Loch Katrine, the loop area was used for quarrying and mining, resulting in a disfigured landscape.

In the 1950s and 1960s, the nearby Gorbals area entered times of great change, with wholesale clearance of its crowded slums. The gaping holes at Cuningar were a convenient location to dump the rubble. Not long afterwards, the grim modern high-rise buildings that had replaced the old tenements were themselves demolished, with the detritus also ending up at Cuningar. Then, in a happy ending, along came the Forestry Commission with many thousands of tonnes of topsoil, some 15,000 saplings and the vision to create an urban woodland.

Covering an area equivalent to 15 football pitches, this kink on the Clyde now boasts an adventure playground, a cycle skills track and an outdoor bouldering park. An array of specially commissioned sculpture begins at the striking entrance gateway. The extensive path network features a riverside boardwalk. There are picnic areas and a small café. Wildlife abounds, and visitors can hope to spot ducks, herons, buzzards, bats, foxes, deer and otters.

The northern end of the loop is a good place to view the legacy of Glasgow's successful hosting of the 2014 Commonwealth Games. On the north bank of the Clyde there was once heavy industry. Today, across a new footbridge, is the village created for the athletes, now a public housing estate. The impressive Emirates Arena and Sir Chris Hoy Velodrome loom large on the skyline, along with Celtic Park football stadium.

Address Downiebrae Road, G75 1PW, +44 (0)300 067 6700, www.scotland.forestry.gov.uk |
Getting there Buses 18, 46, 65, 89, 90, 263 to Downiebrae Road; train to Rutherglen or
Dalmarnock | Hours Daily 7.30am – 5.30pm; for hours of the Wee Cabin Café, check their
Facebook page | Tip Tickets are usually scarce for matches at Paradise, as Celtic Park
football stadium is known. However, there is an interesting walk around the Celtic Way and
a tour that includes the bulging trophy room. You will be told how the 'Bhoys' became the
first British team to win the European Cup.

33 The Cup Tea Lounge

A wally good experience

Much of Glasgow's finest art is hidden. The communal interiors of many of its old residential tenements are exquisitely decorated with glazed tiles, mosaic floors and stained glass. This is the phenomenon of the wally close. In Glaswegian, 'close' means the common entrance and stairway of a building, and 'wally' is a word used for various things made of china. There remains a social cachet about living in a wally close, particularly if the decoration extends beyond the hallway and continues all the way up the stairwell. The hierarchy goes from plain tiles with a coloured border, through those with more elaborate motifs, to panoramic ceramic landscapes and seascapes.

Hyndland, Partick, North Kelvin and Pollokshields are some of the richest areas for wally closes. Today they are all behind locked doors, though it is possible to have up-close encounters on occasional Doors Open Days. Otherwise, the Tenement House (see ch. 103) has a simple and elegant tiled stairway, and Glasgow's museums have many examples of rescued ceramic art, including the work of James Duncan, who designed tiled panels for hundreds of city shops.

One of the city's most glorious tiled interiors can however be studied at your leisure, for the price of a pot of one of their 48 varieties of tea. The Cup Tea Lounge occupies the ground floor of a building designed in 1888 by Alfred Waterhouse for the Prudential Assurance Company. In the 1950s, for reasons known only to the philistines involved, its tiled walls and pillared archways were boxed in behind plasterboard, as the rooms were turned into mundane office space. When the premises were converted into a bar and restaurant in the 1980s, the designers had the simple task of bringing the palatial interior back into the light. It is now a tearoom by day and an upmarket gin joint by night, but first and foremost it is still a place of Victorian splendour.

Address 71 Renfield Street, G2 1LP, +44 (0)141 353 2959, www.cuptearooms.co.uk & www.gin71.com | **Getting there** Short walk from George Square; subway to Buchanan Street | **Hours** Cup Tea Lounge: Mon–Sat 9am–5pm, Sun 11am–5pm; Gin 71: daily 5pm–midnight | **Tip** Any exploration of Glasgow's grand Victorian interiors should include the City Chambers in George Square (free tours Mon–Fri 10.30am & 2.30pm; phone +44 (0)141 287 4018 for information).

34 The Doulton Fountain

A quick spin around the British Empire

Glasgow has many Victorian memorials to the imperial greatness of Britain, most of them stridently militaristic in nature. In the late 19th century it was entirely acceptable to celebrate the invasion and subjugation of far-off lands and the theft of their natural resources. The Doulton Fountain is on a grand scale: at 46 feet high with a 70-foot-wide basin, it is the largest fountain in the world made in terracotta.

The fountain is undoubtedly an object of beauty, but the intent of its creators to achieve grandeur is compromised by an element of caricature, verging on the comic to modern eyes. The bottom tier consists of groups of figures depicting representatives from the four corners of the empire – Australia, South Africa, Canada and India. It is all very stereotypical. The trouble is that the Boer farmer with his ostrich looks like the twin brother of the Australian farmer with his sheep. The Canadian trapper, with moose head in his arms and beaver at his feet, looks a bit bloodthirsty, but the Indian in his turban is majestic.

Each nationality is accompanied by a regal woman, clutching produce depicting the plenitude of the empire, and the upper tier is adorned with four heroic female water-carriers. But none of them is as regal or as heroic as Empress Victoria herself, larger than life at the very top. In 1891, not long after the fountain had been completed, Victoria's likeness was destroyed by lightning – perhaps a judgement on the vainglory of the project – and had to be replaced.

By the 1980s, the fountain was in a neglected and near derelict state due to vandalism and, probably, some Glaswegians helping themselves to pieces of terracotta artwork for their mantelpieces. As part of the city's resurgence of civic pride, the fountain was fully restored, and in 2004 it was moved to a more secure site in Glasgow Green, opposite the People's Palace.

Address Glasgow Green, G40 1AT | Getting there Buses 18, 64, 263 to Green Street or 2, 40, 60, 61, 240, 255 to Bain Street | Hours Unrestricted | Tip The McLennan Arch at the Saltmarket entrance to Glasgow Green is Glasgow's mini Arc de Triomphe. The small triumph is that although the city has demolished many fine buildings, it has also saved some bits, including this centrepiece salvaged from the neoclassical Assembly Rooms.

35 Drygate
Crafty, curious and creative

Until you've visited the Urban Market at Drygate, you probably didn't know that you needed a crocheted cactus or a pair of earrings made of small pencils. This is not your average sprawling outdoor flea market with a jumble of bric-a-brac. It is 'curated', which means that the traders go through a selection process. The result is a collection of designers, artists, artisans and generally inventive people who specialise in the curious and the creative.

There is little in the way of second-hand goods. It is more about upcycling than recycling; one artisan trader makes furniture and household items out of old whisky barrels. Mid-century antiques – tables, chairs, lamps and home appliances from the 1930s to the 1960s that granny might have used – are refurbished for modern use. In a more contemporary vein are the fashion accessories crafted from broken skateboards. Unusual practical goods that may be on sale include dinner services decorated with skeletal imagery, bringing a whole new meaning to bone china, and pocket sandalwood combs, for that awkward social moment when the hipster beard is dishevelled and in need of repair.

There is a lot of edible artistry, with cakes, chocolate and other comestibles, including gin marmalade to pep up the breakfast toast. This is appropriate considering where the Urban Market is held. The Drygate Brewing Co. is described as an experimental venture. It is a joint initiative between craft beer innovators Williams Bros. and Tennent's, Glasgow's biggest brewery, with a history going back to 1571. Much more than brewing goes on here. The Drygate restaurant, with its occasionally sunny terrace, offers rustic food as well as a bewildering range of beers. There is a programme of live music and all kinds of other events, including the Braw Beard and Moustache Championships. Brewery tours and brew-your-own sessions are also available.

Address 85 Drygate, G4 0UT, +44 (0)141 212 8815, www.drygate.com | Getting there Short walk from Glasgow Cathedral; buses 90, CB1 to Drygate or 41 to John Knox Street | Hours Daily 11am–midnight; Urban Market: first and third Sun of the month, noon–5pm; brewery tours: Sun 1pm, 3pm, 5pm. See website for details of events | Tip Pop round the corner to Duke Street and view the murals at Tennent's Brewery, which also has a visitor centre.

36__Empire Coffee Police Box

Who's up for a spicy latte?

To understand the mystique of the police box it is necessary to travel back in time. In the days before two-way radio and mobile phones, these combined telephone kiosks and miniature police stations were a vital cog in the workings of the constabulary. When the light on the roof was flashing it meant that police on patrol should contact the station for an urgent message. Police officers also used the boxes for the temporary detention of suspects, for brewing a cup of tea and for sheltering from the rain.

Glasgow used to have more than 300 police boxes. Only a very few have been saved for posterity and renovated for other uses, such as coffee kiosks. Younger people recognise the boxes as the Tardis from *Doctor Who*, the long-running science-fiction series on BBC television. Used by the doctor for his journeys through time and space, the Tardis is small on the outside but vast inside. At the Empire Coffee box near Glasgow Cathedral, barista and chef Rocco Conforti achieves miracles almost on a Time Lord scale within his tiny, 2.25-square-metre kitchen.

His highly rated choice of coffees includes affogato (espresso with vanilla ice cream) in summer, and spicy latte among the winter warmers. The Mexican hot chocolate is a suitable antidote for a chilly Glasgow day. Highlights of the food menu are sumptuous sandwiches such as the St Mungo (mature cheddar, honey roast ham and caramelised onion chutney) and the Imperial, with roast peppers, hummus and mixed leaves. A bacon roll with a cup of tea is a more traditional Glasgow option. The box also acts as an unofficial tourist information centre, as Rocco manages to find time between the coffee and sandwiches to dish out advice, maps and directions in a chatty, friendly manner.

Address Cathedral Square, G4 0RH, +44 (0)7547 628158 | Getting there Buses 19, 19A, 38, 38B, 38C, 38E, 57, 57A to Glebe Street | Hours Mon–Fri 8am–3.30pm, Sat 9am–3am (phone to check hours in winter) | Tip The ex-police box at the junction of Sauchiehall Street and Renfield Street is now the CBD, or Cannabidiol Hemp Dispensary. To the disappointment of those seeking a high, none of the products on sale contains THC, the ingredient that makes cannabis criminal. The hemp-based oils, tinctures, medicines and foodstuffs in the police box are all legal.

37 — The EVIIIR Postboxes
The king lives on

Britain's iconic red pillar boxes have become a familiar and well-loved part of the streetscape. The Post Office introduced the idea of street collection in 1852, during the reign of Queen Victoria, when the practice of sending letters was becoming no longer the sole preserve of the well-off. The boxes were inscribed with the initials VR, for Victoria Regina. In keeping with the prestige of the Royal Mail, postboxes ever since have been decorated with the cipher of the monarch on the throne at the time of their installation.

In the same way that some people go trainspotting or brass rubbing in old churches, there are those devoted to the study of postboxes. Of particular interest to many postbox aficionados is the time of King Edward VIII. Edward succeeded his father George V in January 1936, but abdicated in December of the same year. He chose to defy convention and marry his love, American divorcée Wallis Simpson, rather than continue with his job as King of the United Kingdom, Emperor of India and ruler of other bits of planet Earth. During the 325 days of his reign, 161 pillar boxes were installed with the inscription EVIIIR. These are considered a rarity among Britain's estimated 115,000 postboxes, and excited enthusiasts will travel hundreds of miles to admire and photograph them. Which is good news for the Glasgow tourist industry since, by a quirk of fate, the disproportionately large number of 27 of these were installed in the city. While the symbol on many of the errant King Edward's boxes was later altered to GVIR, for his successor George VI, Glasgow has about 20 originals still in use.

A compact trail round a choice selection of the EVIIIR postboxes of Hillhead may be followed for about a mile from the one pictured at 64 Great George Street, past another at 9 Crown Road South and on to a third at 70 Hyndland Road. Sounds like paradise for postbox-spotters.

Address 64 Great George Street, G12 8RP | **Getting there** Buses 8, 8A, 90, 372 to Roxburgh Street; subway to Hillhead | **Tip** Glasgow's grand city centre post offices have been converted for other purposes. The office at 47 St Vincent Street, G2 5QX, has swapped stamps for steaks and is now the eye-catching Miller & Carter restaurant. The Letter Box Study Group has information on all the EVIIIR postboxes, and on every other postbox in the UK (www.lbsg.org).

38_Fairfield Heritage

From farmyard to world's biggest shipyard

The River Clyde is the place that launched 30,000 ships. In the early 1900s, its nearly 50 shipyards made one-fifth of the world's entire annual output. At the heart of this great industry was Fairfield in Govan. Begun on farmland in 1849, the yard grew to be the largest and most successful on the Clyde, turning out mighty battleships, luxury passenger liners, and everything else from cargo vessels to ferries. The first vessels down the Fairfield slipway were four fast steamships constructed for the Confederate states during the American Civil War. In 1880, the yard built an opulent steam yacht, the *Livadia*, for Tsar Alexander II. At the launch, his naval adviser Admiral Popoff declared, 'Govan is the centre of intelligence of the world.'

The story of this amazing shipyard is told in the splendid Victorian edifice that was Fairfield's headquarters. The Clyde's mastery of shipbuilding stemmed from its access to steel and iron from Scotland's industrial heartland. A key factor in its success was the ingenuity of its marine engineers, such as Fairfield men David Elder and William Pearce. One display tells of the relationship between bosses and workforce through their respective headgear. The management wore middle-class bowler hats. The 'bunnet' was the flat cloth cap worn by welders, rivetters and other trades. James Bond star Sean Connery took on the role of director only once, in 1967, to make a documentary inspired by Fairfield, *The Bowler and the Bunnet* (see ch.13).

Fairfield survives as one of Glasgow's two remaining shipyards. It has had a succession of new owners including Kvaerner, whose management, wearing industrial hard hats rather than bowlers, tried to encourage the 'bunnets' to work faster. One of them responded, 'This is a boiler suit I'm wearing, no' a tracksuit.' Apart from ships, the Glasgow yards' other famous product was humour.

Address 1048 Govan Road, G51 4XS, +44 (0)141 445 5866, www.fairfieldgovan.org.uk |
Getting there Buses 23, 26 to War Memorial; subway to Govan; ferry (free) from
Riverside Museum (summer only), see www.getintogovan.com/visit | **Hours** Mon–Fri
1–4pm | **Tip** A Govan lad called Alex Ferguson started his working career as an
engineering apprentice. He played football for Rangers, the local team, but is better
known as the legendary manager of Manchester United. As yet there is no celebratory
plaque in his name.

39 Fossil Grove

Wondrous wee petrified forest

Glasgow's oldest attraction dates back some 325 million years. In a corner of Victoria Park, one of the city's loveliest wide-open spaces, is the Fossil Grove. A walk along some eerie and atmospheric pathways in an old quarry leads to a group of petrified stumps of the long extinct *Lepidodondren*, remnants of an ancient forest. Opinion is split on whether the fossils were similar to giant club mosses or more akin to quillworts. This argument is best left to the experts. Just gaze in wonder at a small piece of planet Earth that is mind-bogglingly old.

This Site of Special Scientific Interest was discovered in 1887 when the park was being created. The importance of the fossils was quickly recognised, and a pavilion was constructed to protect them in situ – a move hailed as one of the earliest examples of geoconservation in Britain.

The Fossil Grove landscape was shaped during the Carboniferous Era, those many millions of years when the location now known as Glasgow was on a coastal plain near the equator, with a humid, tropical climate. Fast-forward to 15,000 years ago, and a kilometre-high mountain of ice covered the land. The Glasgow weather is now somewhere between those extremes, going through what might be described as the Dreich Era. ('Dreich' is a Scots word meaning dreary that perfectly describes the cool, damp, overcast weather that all too often persists, despite occasional warm and sunny spells.)

After a stroll down palaeontological memory lane, sample the other delights of Victoria Park. The imposing maroon and gold cast-iron entrance gates lead into a peaceful tree-lined avenue. A lamp post clock with four faces, dating from 1888, is a quaint curiosity. The large pond, once popular with model boat enthusiasts, is home to swans. The play area has a hidden miniature maze where children can be heard but not seen. Restful formal floral displays abound.

Address Victoria Park Drive South, G14 9NW, +44 (0)141 959 9087, www.glasgow.gov.uk | Getting there Buses 1, 1B, 1C, 1D, 1E, 304, 308, 313, 351, 359, 360, 378, 395 to Lime Street | Hours Fossil Grove: Apr–Oct, Sat & Sun noon–4pm; Victoria Park: accessible 24 hours | Tip The Sisters Restaurant, 1a Ashwood Gardens, G13 1NU, specialises in rustic Scottish fare and has a small ivy-clad terrace (+44 (0)141 434 1179, www.thesisters.co.uk, closed Sun).

40__Gardner Street

Hillwalking without leaving the city

Scotland is a paradise for climbers and ramblers. But for those not enamoured of the great outdoors, Glasgow offers the opportunity to go hillwalking without leaving the comforts of the urban environment. The city is built on a series of hills, lumps of glacial debris and glaciomarine sediment gouged out of the landscape during the Ice Age. These small but numerous lumps are called drumlins. The drumlins are oval and elongated with a gentle slope leading to a blunt descent. But that's enough geology. Visitors will quickly realise why so many of the city's districts and street names include the word 'hill'. One area where you can experience hillwalking in the city is Garnethill, where several short streets on precipitous slopes reach northwards from Sauchiehall Street, near Charing Cross.

Further west is one of Glasgow's best-loved drumlins, Gardner Street, with its view over the cityscape of Partick, down towards the River Clyde. Sadly, the view of the riverside is now blocked by a huge and ugly block of apartments for students – just one of the hundreds of luxurious buildings in the city now devoted to accommodating the college generation. (Whatever happened to living in a garret?)

Gardner Street is particularly pretty when covered in snow, but it is not suitable for skiing down, or indeed cycling down, due to its very steep gradient. At its summit is Partickhill Road, which has some of the city's nicest old mansion houses, with spectacular gardens. These occasionally have public open days as part of the charitable Scotland's Gardens scheme.

At the foot of Gardner Street is the bustling working-class shopping area of Dumbarton Road. As well as a world-class concentration of charity shops, Dumbarton Road and its side streets have a thriving collection of small traders, local pubs and cafés, and there is a farmers' market in nearby Mansfield Square.

Address Gardner Street, G11 5BZ | **Getting there** Buses 2, 3, 8, 17, 77, 89, 90 to Partick Library; subway to Partick; Gardner Street leads north opposite 315 Dumbarton Road | **Tip** Roastit Bubbly Jocks at 450 Dumbarton Road is a highly rated restaurant, offering modern Scotttish cuisine such as king scallops, Stornoway black pudding and Dingwall haggis, neeps and tatties – ideal after a spot of hillwalking in the city.

41 Garnethill Synagogue

Kosher tartan and Jewish bagpipers

There is no doubt about the huge contribution that Jewish citizens have made to Glasgow. But how have generations of Jews taken to being Scottish? Wholeheartedly, to judge by the founding of the Jewish Lads Brigade Pipe Band, to say nothing of the three officially-registered Jewish tartans, a general liking for Burns Suppers, and involvement in the whisky industry. The Scottish Jewish Archive Centre, housed at Garnethill Synagogue, provides details of all of these, plus much more solid evidence of a community that has preserved its traditions whilst adopting notable local traits.

The splendid Garnethill Synagogue was designed in 1879 by a local architect, in opulent Moorish style. It is a far cry from the first makeshift Glasgow synagogue, in the back of a High Street shop. The focus of the community soon moved to the south side, where thousands who had fled the Russian pogroms shared overcrowded Gorbals tenements with economic refugees from the Highlands, Ireland, Italy and other troubled parts of the world. Through hard work the Glasgow Jews not only prospered but enriched the city in culture, education, socialist politics, architecture and many other fields.

Jewish immigration came to Glasgow in three waves: first, some two centuries ago, for the commercial opportunities in a booming economy, then to escape oppression in Eastern Europe and later, in the 1930s, to seek safety from the impending horrors of the Holocaust. Scotland is one of the few countries where there has been no state persecution of Jews. This is not just because its own divided Christian populace have been busy antagonising each other for so long: it may also be due to a Scottish characteristic of helping those at risk in an unfriendly world.

Garnethill Synagogue and Archive Centre extends a welcome to all. And you don't have to be Jewish to buy a *kippah* (skullcap) in Shalom tartan.

Address 129 Hill Street, G3 6UB, +44 (0)141 332 4151, www.garnethill.org.uk | **Getting there** Buses 6, 6A, 10A to Stow College; subway to Cowcaddens; train to Charing Cross, then a steep walk up Garnet Street | **Hours** Tours by appointment: email info@sjac.org.uk; check website for details of open days and concerts | **Tip** The one place left to savour kosher cuisine in the Glasgow area is Mark's Deli at 6 Burnfield Road, Giffnock, G46 7QB (Mon–Wed 8am–5pm, Thu 8am–6pm, Fri & Sun 8am–3pm, +44 (0)141 638 8947).

42 — Garthamlock Water Tower

Mind-blowing circle in the sky

You don't have to be a member of the British Water Tower Appreciation Society (motto: 'Onwards and upwards') to be impressed by this vast concrete structure in the East End. Consider it not as a public utility but as a work of art. Admire its slender elegance and unearthly dominance of the landscape. Add imagination and it becomes an intriguing cultural icon. Is it a monumental sculpture that has unaccountably never won an award? A massive brazier for the world's biggest Olympic flame, waiting for Glasgow to be host city of the Games? A giant Zoroastrian Tower of Silence (where Parsee people leave corpses for ecological recycling by scavenger birds), curiously set in a Glasgow housing scheme? Its design has been described as 'futuristic and aspirational'. The later addition of mobile phone masts at the top is at best regrettably functional.

Civil engineering aficionados will be inspired by the vital statistics. The tower is the largest in Britain, with a capacity of 4.5 million litres. Though over 30 metres high, it is only Britain's second-tallest water tower (but height is not everything). Along with its adjacent smaller sibling, the Craigend Tower, it was one of a series dotted throughout Glasgow in the 1950s and 1960s to supply pure, soft Loch Katrine drinking water to the city's many peripheral public housing estates.

The Garthamlock and Craigend Towers have been illuminated as a community arts project and as part of a festival celebrating East End heritage. They are still bathed in light on occasion, beacons of warmth on the night skyline, visible from the M8 motorway and other city vantage points. Close-up viewing of the gleaming concrete circle in the sky is equally rewarding, and more comfortably achieved during daylight hours.

Address Junction of Jerviston Road and Otterswick Place, G33 5QQ | **Getting there** Buses 38, 38A to Tattershall Road or X19 to Inishail Road | **Tip** Break your journey back to the city centre with a stop in Dennistoun, for a walk in Alexandra Park and a visit to Celino's award-winning Italian restaurant and deli at 620 Alexandra Parade, G31 3BT (+44 (0)141 554 0523, www.celinos.com).

43 George Square

The madness of the statues

Glasgow's civic square is named after George III, the monarch best known for losing Britain's American colonies and for having mental health issues. A slight problem is that the city does not quite know what do with its *grande place*. Its role as a focal point for great occasions is hampered by the fact that the square is overpopulated by dead Victorians. To choose one at random, opposite the City Chambers is a statue of James Oswald, a member of parliament for Glasgow from 1832 to 1847, and one of many Oswalds to be MPs. The family were rich merchants whose fortune was based on expertise in the African slave trade.

Oswald's statue was installed in George Square on the insistence of his family and friends, who described him as 'an honourable man'. Another view was expressed some years later by Robert Cunninghame Graham, a socialist MP and founder of both the Labour Party and the Scottish National Party. He was arrested for shouting abuse at Oswald's statue whilst on a night out with the writer Joseph Conrad.

Glasgow City Council had a recent 'strategy' to transform George Square. This involved moving Robert Burns and other dead poets, the steam engine inventor James Watt, a couple of generals from forgotten wars, former prime ministers and a young Queen Victoria, plus her consort Prince Albert and their horses, to 'appropriate places of honour'. Even the square's 80-foot-high column and centrepiece, with its statue of Sir Walter Scott, the historical novelist and re-inventor of the kilt, was to be relocated to 'a point of regeneration'. The project was badly handled by the council, and it came to nothing. It might have worked if they had put Burns up on the big column, found alternative homes for all the rest, and commissioned a new statue of the eponymous monarch, who became quite popular as a result of the movie *The Madness of King George III*.

Address George Square, G2 1DU | Getting there Buses 6, 6A, 15, 18, 41, 100, 500; subway to Buchanan Street; train to Queen Street | Tip George Square is a popular place for picnics. Get yourself a takeaway steak slice (vegetarian options are also available) and a cup of tea from Gregg's on the corner of Queen Street.

44 The Glad Café
Go south for world music

The Glad Café is very much more than a café. It is a cultural institution. This award-winning social enterprise venue in a converted Southside printworks is noted for the excellent variety of its music, visual arts, film and drama programming. It is a home for philosophical talks, political discourse and the great Glasgow tradition of conversation. And, yes, it also offers tasty and innovative food.

The venue attracts audiences from far, wide and even near, as folk from the West End, who used to think that a visa was required to travel south of the river, go for a Glad experience. One of its delights can be sampled on the first Sunday of each month at Sammy's free open-mic music night. The multi-skilled resident band and collection of talented performers will convince you that the Beatles, Beach Boys and Janis Joplin have all come along to entertain. Guests from overseas often bring the house down, though there is the occasional uncertain moment when one of the performers says, 'And here is a song I wrote myself.'

The programme of reasonably priced concerts can truly be described as eclectic. One recent performer was the acclaimed piper and rapper Griogair Labhruidh, whose influences include Gaelic poetry, African rhythms and hip-hop music. Donald Lindsay, a local musician and designer of the world's first 3D-printed bagpipes, demonstrated this wonder at a Glad Café concert. An example of the international flavour is Emily Maguire, a classically trained multi-instrumentalist who lived for years in a shack in the Australian bush, and financed her early career by making goat's cheese.

Do not be put off by a recent press description of the Glad Café as 'the hippest place in Glasgow'. It is definitely cool but it's also down to earth, with the worthy mission of using profits to provide affordable music lessons for local people, so that the fun will flourish.

Address 1006A Pollokshaws Road, G41 2HG, +44 (0)141 636 6119, www.thegladcafe.co.uk | Getting there Buses 3, 38, 38B, 38C, 38E, 57, 57A to Queen's Park | Hours Mon–Wed 9am–11pm, Thu–Sun 10am–midnight | Tip The Shed, directly across Pollokshaws Road, is one of Glasgow's liveliest nightclubs (www.shedglasgow.com).

45 — Glasgow Cross
Unicorns, executions and dancing girls

At what used to be the heart of Glasgow stands a small octagonal building, the Mercat Cross, once a symbol of prosperity, a place for proclamations and civic business. Like market crosses all over Scotland it is topped with a unicorn, the country's national animal. For some reason Scotland adopted as its symbol a mythical medieval beast that never really existed. And Glasgow's cross is itself a piece of make-believe. The original Mercat Cross was demolished in 1659. The copy that was put in place in 1930 has largely been ignored by the public, apart from the unemployed, who used to congregate there to pass their idle days.

The adjacent Tolbooth Steeple is however the real thing. Dating from 1626, it was part of Glasgow's town hall and prison. It was the scene of public executions, torturing of alleged witches, the burning of at least one religious martyr and other such entertainments popular in the 17th century. There were lighter moments, such as when inmates of the debtors' prison would hang shoes out of the windows, begging for money to alleviate their impecunity.

Most of the last of the historic buildings at Glasgow Cross were torn down in 1921 to make way for 'improvements', leaving the steeple as an unlikely adornment on a traffic island. There were plans to knock it down as well, but it was saved by public protest. Glaswegians used to gather there on Hogmanay (New Year's Eve) to listen to the sweet tunefulness of the carillon bells. The steeple remains, but lies unused and silent.

With its pillars and imperious balcony, the Mercat Building – part of the improvements – looks just the place for proclamations and civic events. But it is only an office block. Latterly, one of the tenants on the ground floor was a menswear shop called Krazy House, which achieved notoriety (and some popularity) in the 1970s, by employing scantily clad girls who danced in cages.

Address Junction of High Street, Gallowgate, London Road, Saltmarket and Trongate |
Getting there Buses 2, 18, 60, 60A, 61, 64, 240, 255, 263 to Glasgow Cross | Tip Nearby
at 16 Blackfriars Street, G1 1PE, Babbity Bowster is a legendary Merchant City pub/
restaurant/inn with quality drink, a French chef, regular traditional music sessions and
a nicely cheeky owner called Fraser.

46 Glasgow Museums Resource Centre

In search of hidden treasures

Less than 2 per cent of the 1.5 million or so items held by Glasgow's museums and art galleries are on show at any given time. Uniquely in the UK, the city welcomes visitors to go treasure hunting in the vast hidden world of its stores. The Resource Centre, or GMRC, has 17 'pods' devoted to collections ranging from archaeology, through fine art, to weapons and armour. By advance arrangement, small groups can have a guided tour with one of the knowledgeable specialist curators. Or an individual may ask to see one particular painting from the world-class art collection.

The natural history pod will have visitors of all ages gasping in amazement. A zebra stands beside a herd of various antelopes, untroubled by a nearby tiger. A young giraffe 'grazes' safe from a leopard, which is 200 years old and lives in a glass case. A dozen or so gorgeous owls perched together on a shelf, and a red-bellied toucan, are among the sights to delight the bird spotter. The thousands of residents have been preserved for posterity, or stuffed, to use more prosaic terminology. Some of the older exhibits date from times when shooting exotic wildlife was regarded as normal. Other inmates were sent to the museum taxidermy department from zoos or private collections after dying of natural causes, if such a term can be applied to animals kept in such places. There is a mixture of pathos and wonderment as you gaze upon a young polar bear or a baby gorilla that is beyond cute.

Education and research is a big part of the GMRC programme and a specialist might, for instance, come to study the 100,000 molluscs kept in storage. There is also fun, especially for the young, in a variety of free drop-in events covering topics such as bugs, birds' eggs, dinosaurs, ancient Egypt and pirates.

Address 200 Woodhead Road, G53 7NN, +44 (0)141 276 9300, beta.glasgowlife.org.uk |
Getting there Train to Nitshill from Central Station, then 5-minute walk | **Hours** Mon–Thu
& Sat 10am–5pm, Fri & Sun 11am–5pm; contact GMRCbookings@glasgowlife.org.uk |
Tip A short walk along Nitshill Road to Corselet Road leads to the Dams to Darnley
Country Park. This lesser-known park is a relatively untamed landscape of varied habitats,
with wildlife including roe deer, herons and sometimes too many dog walkers
(www.damstodarnley.org).

47 — Glasgow Tower
Like a candle in the wind

As the 21st century approached, Glasgow, like most cities, was look-ing for a prestigious project to mark the millennium. And so it was decided to build an amazing tower. There was an element of senti-mentality involved, harking back to the Tait Tower, centrepiece of the great Empire Exhibition of 1938 held at the city's Bellahous-ton Park. With Glasgow's engineering and steel moguls behind the project, architect Thomas Tait's Art Deco structure was prefabricated and then put in place in only nine weeks. The 91.44-metre tower was an instant wonder. During the exhibition, 1.3 million people paid to go up it to view the city and its surroundings. The Tait Tower would have remained a landmark had it not been for the outbreak of war. With fears that it would act as a marker for enemy bombers, it was demolished in 1939.

The new Glasgow Tower, beside the Science Centre on the south bank of the Clyde, was to be an even more ambitious and stunning structure. At 127 metres high, it would be the world's tallest building that rotated fully 360 degrees. The tower has indeed become famous, but not entirely for the right reasons. Glasgow's coat of arms features 'the fish that never swam and the bird that never flew'. Now the city has the rotating tower that does not rotate very often. Serious technical issues meant that it had to close in February 2002, just five months after it opened, and for the following 12 years it was operational only 20 per cent of the time.

The good news is that since 2014 the Glasgow Tower has been back in business, and absolutely safe for visitors to ascend and enjoy the wonderful views. The irony is that although its sail shape is designed to rotate gently in the wind, it has been decided that it will not operate when gusts exceed 25 miles per hour, as they often do in the exposed riverside location. So try to choose a calm day for your visit.

Address 50 Pacific Quay, G51 1DA, +44 (0)141 420 5000, www.glasgowsciencecentre.org |
Getting there Buses 23, 23A, 23B, 26, X19 to Pacific Drive | Hours Apr–Oct, daily
11am–4.30pm | Tip The Science Centre itself has displays demonstrating fascinating
applications of engineering and technology, more successful than the rotating tower
(Apr–Oct, daily 10am–5pm; Nov–Mar, Wed–Fri 10am–3pm, Sat & Sun 10am–5pm).

48 Glasgow's Dalí

Buying art at a Scottish price

Glasgow has one of the finest and most extensive civic art collections in Europe. Its roll call of works by the likes of Rembrandt, Van Gogh, Degas, Gauguin and Matisse were mainly bequeathed to the city by wealthy industrialists with a penchant for collecting fine art. But its favourite painting, *Christ of St John of the Cross* by Salvador Dalí, was obtained through some good, old-fashioned Scottish haggling.

Dr Tom Honeyman was a Glasgow GP who gave up medicine to become a successful art dealer in London, before returning to take up the relatively poorly paid post of director of the city's art galleries, a role he pursued with great dynamism. In 1951, Honeyman used his skills to persuade Dalí to sell his striking painting of the crucified Christ to the city at the knock-down price of £8,200 – and to hand over the reproduction rights. The cost (which was still considerable) was quickly recouped as Glaswegians queued in their thousands at Kelvingrove Art Gallery and paid sixpence each to view the controversial purchase. Over the decades the painting has paid for itself many times over through the sale of postcards, prints and posters. Dalí was reportedly miffed about the low price, but not enough to affect his friendship with Honeyman. *Christ of St John of the Cross* became the most popular work in the Glasgow collection, and it is constantly in demand to go on loan all over the world. In 2006, the Spanish government tried to buy it for £80 million.

Despite his success in raising Glasgow's art profile internationally and increasing attendances at the Kelvingrove Gallery, Honeyman was eventually deposed from his post as director by small-minded council politicians. But not before he had persuaded Sir William Burrell, a shipping magnate and magpie collector of art, in the style, if not on the scale, of William Randolph Hearst, to leave his vast collection to the city.

Address Kelvingrove Art Gallery and Museum, Argyle Street, G3 8AG,
+44 (0)141 276 9599, beta.glasgowlife.org.uk | Getting there Buses 2, 3, 17, 77, 100 to
Kelvingrove; subway to Kelvinhall | Hours Mon–Thu & Sat 10am–5pm, Fri & Sun
11am–5pm | Tip There is a small but lovely memorial garden to Dr Tom Honeyman
in Kelvingrove Park, with views both of the gallery and of the university where he
studied. You will find it just off Kelvin Way, next to the statue of Joseph Lister.

49 _ Glickman's

Where sweet dreams come true

Glickman's is not just a sweetie shop. It is a time machine, transporting customers of various ages back to their own place in the confectionery space-time continuum. We are not talking here about the Mars Bar, Milky Way or Galaxy of the multinational companies. Founded in 1903 and still going strong, Glickman's is all about local favourites, many of them still made in the back shop according to Isaac Glickman's original recipes, by his granddaughter Irene and her daughter Julie.

The small shop stocks a vast range of delicacies, including the best-selling Candy Balls and Macaroon Cake. The Scottish macaroon has nothing to do with delicate almond biscuits. It is an intensely sweet, solid fondant dipped in chocolate and rolled in toasted coconut. It has a strange connection with Scottish football, as a favourite 'dessert' for spectators after the traditional match snack of a pie with Bovril beef drink. Vendors used to pass through the terracing calling out, 'And it's your Macaroon Bars!' (Spearmint chewing gum was also on offer, possibly to cleanse the palate.) It is a mystery how mashed potato came to be one of its major ingredients.

The Lucky Tattie (lucky potato), another age-old favourite, has no actual potato in it, consisting chiefly of sugar and glucose fused into a chewy lump and dusted with cinnamon. At its centre there was once a lucky charm such as a plastic Scottie dog, but these have now gone, presumably due to modern health and safety concerns.

Not everything is so sweet. The Soor Plooms (sour plums) have a lime-flavoured acidic kick. The melt-in-the-mouth Cough Tablet with aniseed is a blast from the past, when Glasgow's industrial pollution caused widespread respiratory problems. A dentist fan of Glickman's says, 'It's OK to eat sweets in moderation, preferably as a digestive after a meal, followed by a thorough brushing of the teeth.'

Address 157 London Road, G1 5BX, +44 (0)141 552 0880, www.glickmans.co.uk |
Getting there Buses 18, 64, 263 to Charlotte Street | **Hours** Tue–Fri 10am–4pm,
Sat & Sun 10am–5pm | **Tip** Contrary to popular perceptions of the Glasgow diet,
a lot of fruit and vegetables are in fact consumed in the city. For an ample selection of
healthy foods, check out the market-style Roots & Fruits at 457 Great Western Road,
G12 8HH and its organic deli next door.

50 The Govan Stones
Relics of a lost kingdom

The richly worked stones to be seen in the Old Church of Govan are among the finest early medieval monuments in Britain. The antiquity of this whole area is also worthy of consideration. Many centuries ago, when Glasgow was a farming village with a settlement of missionaries seeking converts to Christianity on behalf of Rome, Govan was the seat of power of the ancient Briton kings of Strathclyde. Their domain covered the southern part of what is now Scotland, and their Brythonic connections extended to Wales and northern England.

The stones date from the 9th to the 11th century, when these kings and warrior chieftains were fighting guerrilla actions against invading Vikings. For centuries, the historic artefacts lay unprotected and largely ignored in the graveyard of Govan Old Church. In the 1980s, before the 31 stones on display were taken indoors and given due loving attention, 14 other medieval treasures were destroyed when a wall between the graveyard and a neighbouring shipyard was demolished.

The church, now a visitor centre used only occasionally for services, makes a stunning setting for the stones. Notable amongst the intricate carving are some eye-catching writhing serpents. For eerie effect, the five huge hogback stones take pride of place. These have nothing to do with pigs, though they do resemble scary animals. They may have marked the graves of Briton kings, but historians detect a Scandinavian influence, so perhaps those fearsome Vikings were involved.

Another treasure rescued from the graveyard is the Govan Sarcophagus. This impressive coffin, carved from a large block of sandstone, may have held the remains of Constantine, a missionary who brought Christianity to Govan around 500 A.D., though it is more likely to have been another of that name, the last king of the Picts, who was killed in 878 A.D. fighting the Vikings.

Address 866 Govan Road, G51 RUU, +44 (0)141 440 2466, www.thegovanstones.org.uk | Getting there Buses 23, 26 to War Memorial; subway to Govan; ferry (free) from Riverside Museum (summer only), see www.getintogovan.com/visit | Hours Apr–Oct, daily 1–4pm | Tip Govan now has an eaterie that is a café verging on a bistro. Café 13 at 794 Govan Road, opposite the dreary shopping centre, offers good coffee, great baking, and some interesting dishes in addition to breakfasts and burgers (Mon–Fri 9am–6pm).

51 The Grand Ole Opry

Singers and gunslingers

The roots of American country music owe much to Scottish emigrants, cruelly expelled from their native land during the Highland Clearances. Many found their way to the Appalachian Mountains, taking with them their fiddles, songs and dances. The Scots folk tradition later melded with Irish, English and African influences. The Grand Ole Opry in Nashville, Tennessee has since 1925 been at the centre of America's hugely popular country music culture, with star performers like Johnny Cash, Dolly Parton and Patsy Cline. In 1974, Glasgow's own Grand Ole Opry was set up by local enthusiasts, who transformed a disused cinema into a music venue, creating their own little bit of Nashville.

The melancholy nature of country and western appeals to something deep in the psyche of the Scots. They enjoy a good night out listening to sad songs such as Hank Williams' 'I'm So Lonesome I Could Cry'. That's the one where even a little robin weeps because he has lost the will to live. But it's not just about the music at the Grand Ole Opry. Members buy into the whole deal, wearing stetsons, fancy shirts, boots and other cowboy accoutrements. (This uniform is not compulsory.) The Opry is also home to the Glasgow Gunslingers. Pistol-packing, fast-draw shoot-outs are part of the entertainment. No live ammunition, of course, though there are signs dotted around the club warning 'No guns beyond this point'. Ironically, the gunslingers turn out to be peaceful folk, who may invite visitors to a friendly duel.

Perhaps because of the historical connections between Scotland and the southern states of the USA, there is a lingering fondness for the Confederacy, and commiseration for its defeat in the American Civil War. At the end of evening performances at the Glasgow Opry, there is a ceremonial folding of the Confederate battle flag to the strains of 'I wish I was in Dixie...'

Address 2 Govan Road, G51 1HS, +44 (0)141 429 5396, www.glasgowsgrandoleopry.co.uk |
Getting there Buses 23, 26, 38 to Marine Crescent; subway to Shields Road | Hours Live
music Fri & Sat 7.30–11.30pm; check website for full programme | Tip Across the road
from the Opry, The Old Toll Bar at 1 Paisley Road West is the city's finest example of a
preserved Victorian Glasgow pub. It has been demodernised, with the removal of TV sets,
fruit machines, optics and other non-original features. The service, drink and food all match
the magnificent interiors.

52 Helensburgh Heritage Centre

The John Logie Baird story

The opportunity to see one of the world's earliest televisions is just one of many good reasons to take a trip to the town of Helensburgh, birthplace of John Logie Baird. Baird is variously described as 'the inventor' or 'a pioneer' of television. What is not in doubt is that in 1926 he was the first person to transmit moving images via a TV system. One of the first commercially available receivers, the Televisor, is on display at the Heritage Centre, along with a working replica of an early home-assembly receiver. The name did not catch on, otherwise people today would be asking, 'What's on the televisor tonight?'

Baird's mechanical system, described initially as 'seeing by wireless', was superseded by electronic systems in the 1930s. By that time he was busy inventing colour TV. He advised the BBC to get into colour broadcasting nearly 30 years before they did so. Even as a teenager, Baird was a restless inventor, rigging up a telephone system between houses in his Helensburgh street. He studied engineering in Glasgow before joining the Clyde Valley Electricity Company, where his career was short-circuited when an illicit experiment in making diamonds from graphite ended up disrupting Glasgow's electricity supply.

Baird's inventing continued, and he went on to hold 177 patents. Not all of his inventions were successful. A treatment for haemorrhoids turned out to be more painful than the medical condition. His attempt to revolutionise jam making at a sugar plantation in the Caribbean was a financial failure. He did however achieve commercial success during World War I, with his foot-warming thermal undersock. His continual passionate work on the development of television brought him fame, if not fortune, before his early death in 1946.

Address Helensburgh Library, 51 West King Street, Helensburgh, G84 8EB, +44 (0)1436 658833 | Getting there Train to Helensburgh from Queen Street (45 minutes); the Baird Room is in the Heritage Centre on the upper floor of Helensburgh Library | Hours Mon & Thu 1–8pm, Tue, Wed & Sat 9.30am–5pm (closed 1–2pm), Fri 1–5pm | Tip The Mackintosh Club, housed in an impressive building designed by Charles Rennie of that ilk for the local Conservatives, is now an arts venue with an exhibition celebrating the man and his works (40/2 Sinclair Street, Helensburgh, G84 8SU, +44 (0)1436 674375, www.mackintosh.club).

53 __ Holmwood
What the nuns hid under the wallpaper

Do not visit this historic house expecting great opulence or grandeur. Despite its impressive frontage and fabulous cupola, Holmwood is only a wee bit opulent. It is not on a grand scale, being a big villa rather than a mansion house. But it is rightly described as a house like no other. When Joseph Couper decided in 1856 to build a family home in the countryside near his paper mill in Cathcart, he called upon the services of the prolific and much-in-demand Glasgow architect Alexander 'Greek' Thomson. The clue to Thomson's work is in his nickname. He was inspired by the architectural remains of ancient Greece (as well as of Egypt and Assyria). Glasgow became home to a collection of fine buildings reflecting his 19th-century take on classical style.

As with all his projects, Thomson paid attention to every last detail of the interior design of Holmwood. The dining room, for instance, has a frieze based on illustrations of Homer's *Iliad*.

The Coupers sold Holmwood in 1907, and it became home to a series of families who more or less maintained the 'Greek' ambience. In 1958 it was bought by the Sisters of Our Lady of the Missions and turned into a convent school. The interior underwent drastic changes. The dining room became a chapel, and the frieze, with the odd naked ancient Greek, was deemed unsuitable and painted over. Most of the rest of Thomson's décor was hidden under Anaglypta wallpaper and brown paint.

When the school closed in 1994, Holmwood was sold to a property developer, before the National Trust for Scotland stepped in and saved it for posterity. Holmwood sets the pulse racing for architectural historians. For the lay person there is also much of interest, not least the ongoing painstaking process of restoring and recreating the original interiors, using as a guide a book published in 1868 that contains extensive details of Thomson's designs.

Address 61–63 Netherlee Road, G44 3YU, +44 (0)141 571 0184, www.nts.org/Visit/
Holmwood-House | Getting there Train to Cathcart, then walk down Rhannan Road
to Netherlee Road | Hours Mar–Oct, Fri–Mon noon–5pm (last entry 4pm) | Tip
Visitors can help themselves to surplus produce from Holmwood's vegetable gardens.
Check the website for events, including garden parties in the grounds.

54 Homeless Jesus
At the heart of the city

There used to be a favourite city centre walk known as 'up Sauchie, doon Buckie an' alang Argyle', taking in Glasgow's main shopping thoroughfares of Sauchiehall Street, Buchanan Street and Argyle Street. It started at Charing Cross, a place of architectural grandeur until it was destroyed by a motorway, and finished at the end of Trongate at Glasgow Cross. Stretches of both Sauchiehall and Argyle have seen better days, but Buchanan thrives as the second-busiest shopping street in Britain after Oxford Street in London.

Walking up 'Buckie' will take you past (and probably into) a number of notable retail centres. House of Fraser is a traditional department store, once the headquarters of the Scottish company that owned many of Britain's most famous names, including Harrod's in London. The Parisian-style Argyll Arcade dates from 1827 and houses a curious collection of more than 30 jewellers and diamond merchants under one roof. Princes Square is a lovely covered shopping mall, modernised in 1987, with upmarket shops and restaurants in its elegant upper tiers. At the top of the street are the less lovely Buchanan Galleries, attached to the Stalinist structure of Glasgow Concert Hall.

So where does *Homeless Jesus* figure? At the heart of Buchanan Street is St George's Tron, a prestigious church whose interior is now largely devoted to a haven called the Wild Olive Tree Café, but which is still very much a place of worship in a modern way. Part of its mission is to highlight the plight of the many Glaswegians who live rough on the streets. On the pavement at the rear of the church is a life-size bronze sculpture of a shrouded figure sleeping on a bench. The wounds on the feet give the clue that it is Jesus. In the midst of the celebration of Mammon this artwork, by Canadian sculptor Timothy Schmalz, is a reminder of the less fortunate in society.

Address Nelson Mandela Place, G2 1QY, behind St George's Tron | Getting there Short walk from George Square; subway to Buchanan Street; train to Queen Street | Hours Unrestricted; Wild Olive Tree Café: Mon–Sat 10.30am–4.30pm | Tip Glasgow's other Tron church at 63 Trongate, G1 5HB, is now a lively theatre venue (+44 (0)141 552 4267, www.tron.co.uk).

55 The Horse Shoe Bar

Bring on the pies

The Horse Shoe Bar is doubly protected. It is an A-listed building, which means that any changes to the inside or outside are prohibited by the architecture police. It also has self-appointed guardians, customers who take it upon themselves to preserve this legendary Glasgow pub from those with an itch to modernise.

There has been a pub on this site in Drury Street since 1846, but it was 30 years later that the establishment was transformed into its present glory. Glasgow publican John Scouller took it over and rebuilt it in regal fashion. He renamed it the Horse Shoe, and filled it with horse-themed interior detail such as horseshoe fireplaces, tables and carvings. He had a thing about horses.

Scouller created the vast, curved, continuous island bar for which the pub is renowned. Its shape resembles a huge horseshoe joined to a smaller one. At 104 feet 3 inches long, it is claimed to be the longest such pub counter in the UK, Europe, or maybe the universe, depending on which version you prefer. It is said that Scouller designed it thus and removed the many side rooms so that staff could better keep an eye on what the customers were up to. Apart from drinking, this was mostly enjoying the Horse Shoe's simple fare, like your granny used to make (if she could actually cook). The favourite snack with your pint was a traditional Scotch pie – for the uninitiated, that is a round, double-crust, individual pastry filled with minced mutton.

When the pub was bought by a huge chain that took pies off the menu in favour of modern pub grub, customers formed a resistance movement. The new owners had to admit defeat in the Pie Wars and restore the delicacy. Unfortunately, the new pies were not the genuine Scotch variety from the previous local suppliers. Suffice it to say that the ancient sign proclaiming 'Famous Horse Shoe Pies' has now been taken down. From the pub's extensive menu you can now have a beetroot and quinoa burger with your pint.

Address 17–19 Drury Street, G2 5AE, +44 (0)141 248 6368, www.thehorseshoebarglasgow.co.uk | **Getting there** Short walk from Central Station or George Square; subway to Buchanan Street | Hours Daily 9am–midnight | Tip The Horse Shoe has karaoke each night in the upstairs lounge, as you may hear when you enter Drury Street. It is proof that Glasgow has talent. Be warned – only very good singers, or the tuneless but brave, should dare mount the stage.

56 House for an Art Lover
Toshie is alive and well

Architect, designer and artist Charles Rennie Mackintosh would no doubt have liked to add extra flourishes and detail during the construction of this house. This was not possible, since building began in 1989 and Mackintosh had died in 1928. The design for the building dates back to 1901, when Mackintosh and his artist wife Margaret Macdonald entered a competition launched by a German magazine to design a *Haus eines Kunstfreundes*, or art lover's house. Mackintosh's entry was disqualified because it was incomplete – not the last time he would have problems with competition deadlines. But his design was judged to be of such outstanding quality that he was given 600 German marks for effort, and his portfolio was published.

Nearly 90 years later, Mackintosh was very much there in spirit when a team of Toshie-minded architects, civil engineers, artists and craftworkers gathered to build the house. They had Mackintosh's drawings to work from. Missing details were found with detective work inside Glasgow School of Art and other buildings created by Mackintosh in his prime. The result is a public place that is not just a museum or gallery. The house and its interiors are the artwork. Did Mackintosh succeed with his vision of a decorous place to live? Just a glance at the glorious music room and terrace leaves no doubt.

Experts explain how the house encapsulates the many elements of his style, such as Art Nouveau, Japonisme, Arts and Crafts, Celtic Revival, Symbolism, Vienna Secession and his modern take on the Scottish vernacular. The lay person can simply appreciate how Mackintosh's genius took architecture and design out of the Victorian era into a new age. The House for an Art Lover has spawned an entire village of artistic endeavour in its corner of Bellahouston Park, including a sculpture garden, studios set in a walled garden and an inspired children's playpark.

Address Bellahouston Park, 10 Dumbreck Road, G41 5BW, +44 (0)141 353 4770, www.houseforanartlover.co.uk | Getting there Buses 9, 9A, 10, 38 to Helen Street | Hours Times vary, as the house is used for private events; check website | Tip The Mackintosh House, part of Glasgow University's Hunterian Art Gallery, shows how Mackintosh and his wife Margaret lived themselves, with the interiors saved from their home before it was demolished (82 Hillhead Street, G12 8Q, +44 (0)141 330 5434, www.gla.ac.uk/hunterian; check website for details of opening hours and tours).

57__Hutcheson's Hall

A rich man's poorhouse

Glasgow's most generally lauded architects are Charles Rennie Mackintosh and Alexander 'Greek' Thomson. But before their time the man known as the father of Glasgow architecture, David Hamilton (1786–1843), built large chunks of the Georgian and early Victorian city and also trained the next generation. Hutcheson's Hospital (1802–05) was one of his earliest assignments, a rather grand establishment for its dual role as a school for poor boys and a home for elderly merchants. The two 17th-century statues adorning the building are of brothers George and Thomas Hutcheson, who founded the charitable institution, originally on Trongate, back in 1641.

The school moved long ago to the south of the city, and remains a flourishing fee-paying institution. Hutcheson's Hall has since been a library, banking premises and offices of the National Trust for Scotland. An elegant restaurant is now custodian of the carefully restored building.

Hamilton was a stonemason before emerging as the busiest architect of his era. Within sight of Hutcheson's Hall are his Royal Exchange, now the Gallery of Modern Art, and Ship Bank, now a five-storey pleasure palace called the Corinthian. His portfolio also included a theatre, the Bridge of Sighs at the Necropolis, the Normal School (Britain's first specialist teacher-training college) and many grand houses. In 1835 he came third in the competition to design the Houses of Parliament in London, getting £500 for his efforts.

His fame would later be eclipsed, not only by Mackintosh and Thomson, but by that of his granddaughter Madeleine Smith. In 1857 she was accused, but not convicted, of poisoning her French lover Pierre L'Angelier. She has since been portrayed in books, plays and films as a flirtatious society girl who got away with murder. Recent research revealing L'Angelier as a psychopathic stalker has only added to the mystery.

Address 158 Ingram Street, G1 1EJ, +44 (0)141 553 4050, www.hutchesonsglasgow.com | Getting there Short walk from George Square or Central Station | Hours Mon–Thu noon–2am, Fri & Sat 10am–2am, Sun 10am–1am | Tip David Hamilton's 44-metre-high Nelson Monument stands on Glasgow Green. It was erected in 1806, just a year after the great admiral's victory at Trafalgar and 34 years before London's column.

58 The Kelbourne Saint

Home of hut cuisine

Glasgow's restaurants try hard to offer alfresco dining experiences, which is no easy task for much of the year in a rainy and often chilly climate. The Kelbourne Saint goes beyond the giant umbrellas and portable heaters installed by other venues to combat the cold and wet. In their hidden garden they have built a row of garden sheds kitted out as smart dining rooms. The colourful and comfortable interiors make cosy spaces for a communal eating experience. The huts are fitted with heaters, lighting, power and USB ports. A nice touch is that the space under each table has been converted into a dog kennel. The Kelbourne Saint loves canines, and offers dogs' dinners on its menu.

The centrepiece of Kelbourne Saint cooking is a giant rotisserie. Their free-range chicken is fed a special diet including the same grain used to brew the house beer, which is pumped directly from a huge tank on the ceiling. The chefs will have a go at anything that can be spit-roasted, from octopus to suckling pig. And it's not all meat, with Parmesan and truffle fries, sourdough stack of garlic and truffled wild mushrooms and maple-roasted root vegetables among the options.

The building's original incarnation was a 19th-century church hall – hence the name. It was latterly a bar that had an ugly moment of cinematic fame. Standing in for an Edinburgh location in the film *Trainspotting*, it was used for a violent pub fight scene, when mayhem ensues after the character Begbie casually throws a pint glass from a balcony. But the Kelbourne Saint is no rough Edinburgh pub. It is a hospitable Glasgow West End family local, and an ideal retreat after a walk in the nearby Botanic Gardens. Children are welcome, and there is a playpark in the garden to keep them occupied. There is also a Little Saints menu, so the young ones can eat inexpensive, scaled-down portions of adult dishes.

Address 182 Queen Margaret Drive, G20 8NX, +44 (0)141 946 9456,
www.kelbournesaint.com | Getting there Buses 8, 8A, 90, 372 to Oban Lane; subway
to Hillhead | Hours Daily 11am–midnight | Tip Maryhill Burgh Halls are home to an
extraordinary set of 19th-century stained-glass panels by Stephen Adam, depicting
workers in the many trades once pursued in the area (10–24 Gairbraid Avenue,
G20 8YE; for information on building tours phone +44 (0)845 860 1878 or email
heritage@mbht.org.uk).

59 — Kelvin Hall
A scent of history

Across the road from the imposing Kelvingrove Art Gallery and Museum is a plainer but still handsome red sandstone building that has served Glasgow well for almost a century. The Kelvin Hall was originally built to house large-scale exhibitions, but it has been a versatile location over the years. It was here that Glasgow's most famous boxer, Benny Lynch, defended his world champion titles in the 1930s. In 1955, American evangelist Billy Graham brought religious fervour to Kelvin Hall, preaching to 180,000 people during a six-week run. It was a major concert venue, where a young Elton John appeared in 1972.

Glaswegians reminisce mostly about the annual circus and funfair, usually mentioning the conflicting aromas of candy floss and elephant dung that permeated the building. In the later 20th century, when maltreating wild animals had ceased to be considered entertainment, Kelvin Hall became home to an international indoor athletics stadium and a much-loved transport museum. Now that the city has so many other spanking new sport, concert and exhibition venues, the building has had a splendid makeover. It continues life as a multi-functional space in a collaboration between Glasgow Life, the National Library of Scotland and Glasgow University's Hunterian Museum and Gallery.

Tours are available of the Open Collections, where over 400,000 artefacts from the city's museums are stored. Conservation work can be seen in action. Or you can just wander through an arcade of exhibits, including fine examples from Glasgow's rich history of ceramic tiles. The National Library's outpost in the west offers big-screen and digital access to film and video from its vast Moving Image Archive. On the sporting front, pay-as-you-go membership is available to the state-of-the-art health and fitness club. The only thing missing from the new Kelvin Hall is that old circus aroma.

Address 1445 Argyle Street, G3 8AW, +44 (0)141 276 1450, www.kelvinhall.org.uk | Getting there Buses 2, 3, 17, 77, 100 to Kelvingrove; subway to Kelvinhall | Hours Times vary for different departments – check website for full information; email kelvinhalltours@glasgowlife.org.uk to book Open Collections tours | Tip Number 16 Restaurant at 16 Byres Road, G11 5JY, comes highly recommended for its Scottish cuisine and cosy atmosphere.

60 Kelvingrove Bandstand

Tom Jones on stage? It's not unusual

Glasgow has over 90 parks and public gardens. In the Victorian era, many of these were furnished with elegant bandstands, where citizens could escape from the factories and slum housing to enjoy some alfresco musical entertainment. In the radical era of Red Clydeside, the bandstands also housed May Day rallies and other political events. But over the years, they sadly fell to dereliction and demolition as a result of neglect and vandalism, both individual and corporate.

The sole survivor is the Kelvingrove Park bandstand, which in the later 20th century was a focal point for Glasgow's lively rock music scene, hosting the likes of Hue and Cry, Simple Minds and Wet Wet Wet. Free festivals with up-and-coming bands and community events helped to keep it alive. But lack of maintenance led to its closure in the 1990s, and it appeared to have a date with the bulldozers. A community action group called Friends of Kelvingrove Park decided not to let this happen. Raising awareness and funds, they finally cajoled (some might say shamed) the City Council into saving the bandstand.

After £2.1 million of renovation and improvements, orchestrated by Page\Park architects, the bandstand is back as a community asset. It also has a more secure financial future, as an occasional boutique venue – 2,500 capacity – for intimate concerts by big-name artists. Tom Jones loves the place and has committed himself to annual dates there. Brian Wilson, Sister Sledge and Dr Hook have featured on the roll call of performers. The setting is stunning, enhanced on concert nights by artistic lighting of the trees and river. Canny Glaswegians eschew the purchase of expensive tickets, preferring to listen to the music from the park outside. Some, including ladies of a certain age desperate for a glimpse of Tom Jones, have even tried to get a view into the venue by standing on car roofs.

Address Kelvingrove Park, Kelvin Way, G3 | Getting there Buses 4, 4A, 15, X25A, X76, X77 to University Union, then a short walk along Kelvin Way | Hours See Facebook site of Kelvingrove Bandstand and Amphitheatre for details of concerts | Tip If you are going to a summer gig and the weather is good, you can picnic in the park. There are tables with built-in barbecues a few hundred metres away, beside the Stewart Memorial Fountain.

61 Kelvingrove Lawn Bowling

Fun with odd-shaped balls

There are two great things about the sport of bowls. It's a game for all ages, where a 70-year-old is quite likely to beat a 17-year-old. And in Glasgow you can play free of charge (bowls provided) at the world's top venue, where the 2014 Commonwealth Games were held – when Scotland's men won three out of four gold medals, by the way.

The ancient pursuit of bowls is best remembered by many as the game Sir Francis Drake decided to finish on Plymouth Hoe before going off to defeat the Spanish Armada. The rules of how the sport is played today were set out in 1864 by William Wallace Mitchell, a Glasgow merchant. Not that it's complicated. There can be up to four players in a team. The object is to chuck big balls along the grass towards a smaller white ball. Players get one point for each big ball that ends up closest to the smaller ball. The bowls are radially asymmetrical, which means that one side is slightly ovoid. The main thing to remember, from a skills point of view, is to keep this side, which is marked by a wee dot, to the inside of your chosen curved trajectory.

Glasgow has the largest concentration of private bowls clubs and public greens of any city in the United Kingdom. The sport can be a touch regimented at club level, with rules about blazers and badges. There is also segregation of the sexes. If you're reading up on the subject, don't be confused by references to 'promiscuous pairs competitions'. This is nothing to do with splendour on the grass – they're merely games where players can swap teams.

There is, of course, no segregation on public greens. Behaviour code is simple. Wear flat shoes. No running. No overhand bowling. Don't sit on the grassy bank round the green. Or the 'parkie' (attendant) may have to have a word.

Address Kelvingrove Lawn Bowls & Tennis Centre, Kelvin Way, G3 7TA, +44 (0)7920 048945, www.glasgowlife.org.uk/sport | **Getting there** Buses 2, 3, 17, 77, 100 to Kelvingrove; subway to Kelvinhall | **Hours** Apr–Sept, Mon–Fri 9am–9pm, Sat & Sun 9am–6pm (but these times may vary – phone to check) | **Tip** An Clachan café in Kelvingrove Park, G3 7LH, offers free-range food, fairtrade coffee and a large variety of herbal teas (www.kelvingroveparkcafe.co.uk, +44 (0)7832 485668).

62 King Billy Statue

Glasgow's favourite Orangeman

Here is a man undoubtedly worthy of a statue. William III of England and Ireland, and William II of Scotland, also known as Prince William of Orange, was a notable figure in late 17th-century British history, laying foundations for a parliamentary democracy served by a constitutional monarchy. He did so by deposing his father-in-law James, a deluded soul who believed in the divine right of kings. William was a big player on the European scene as an opponent to Louis XIV of France and his grandiose schemes, occasionally in alliance with the Vatican.

In Glasgow, 'King Billy' is regarded mainly as a symbol of Protestant supremacy. The Orange Order, an organisation that Scotland inherited from its Northern Irish connections, still holds annual parades around 12 July, to mark William's victory in 1690 at the Battle of the Boyne. Opinions are divided on the merits of these Orange walks. Those marching on the streets perceive them as a colourful commemoration, with stirring music, of William's glorious revolution, and an affirmation of Protestant traditions. Others see them as a licence for rampant anti-Catholicism, and a distasteful echo of the sectarian persecution suffered for decades by Irish immigrants. For the many who care neither about the Orange nor the Green, the parades are viewed mainly as the cause of irritating and unnecessary traffic jams.

The memorial, erected in 1735, is something of an enigma. It depicts King Billy as a Roman emperor, which may be regarded as strangely Vaticanesque by his present-day followers. (Orange Order iconography shows him as a bold cavalier astride a white charger.) William once had pride of place near Glasgow Cross. He is now located in a green square near the Cathedral, behind a big iron fence. This prevents close inspection of details such as the horse's articulated tail, which allegedly sways in the wind.

Address Cathedral Square, G4 0QY | **Getting there** Buses 19, 19A, 38, 38B, 38C, 38E, 57, 57A to Glebe Street | **Tip** The imposing and richly adorned blonde sandstone building in Cathedral Square is home to Glasgow Evangelical Church. Features include memorials to local Protestant martyrs and a modern stained-glass window marking the bicentenary of the Orange Order.

63 The Knitted Bench

Memories stitched together

A park bench makes a lovely memorial. It is a place of rest and contemplation for the public, and a source of comfort for grieving family and friends. Most are marked with a simple plaque. Some may be ornately carved. The bench in Glasgow's Botanic Gardens in memory of artist Rita McGurn is quite different, thanks to its colourful woollen overcoat.

Rita was at Glasgow School of Art, but as a model, not a student. She taught herself drawing, painting and sculpture. Her knack of using flamboyant fabrics and vintage furniture before retro became fashionable got her into interior design. Making exotic chandeliers from teaspoons, sherry glasses or anything else that came to hand became a forte. She was in demand as a designer for film, television and theatre, and was involved in virtually every field of artistic endeavour. In her spare time (a concept she did not actually recognise) Rita was an incessant knitter. She created scores of 'soft sculptures', striking figures in wool and papier-mâché, including one that stood 14 feet tall, called *Izal* after the toilet paper from which she was partly constructed.

After Rita died in 2015, her daughter Mercedes was sitting on her favourite bench in the Botanic Gardens, just across the road from the McGurn family home, when she had the idea of creating a Rita-style installation. Mercedes had heard about yarn bombing, the practice of decorating items of street furniture with wool, and got permission from the park authorities to try out the concept there. After a few months of concerted knitting, and considerable help from family and friends, the bench with the coat of many colours made its appearance. It is decorated with small knitted birds, but no big softly sculpted people, so as to leave room for humans. It has brought many smiles. The woolly bench can be seen from March to the end of September, when it goes into hibernation.

Address Botanic Gardens, 730 Great Western Road, G12 0UE, +44 (0)141 276 1614 | **Getting there** Buses 6, 6A, 6B, 8, 8A, 10A, 90, 372 to Botanic Gardens; subway to Hillhead | **Hours** Bench on display Mar–Sept, daily 7am–dusk | **Tip** Near the bench, opposite the entrance to the Children's Garden you will find a twisted hazelnut bush, better known as Harry Lauder's Walking Stick. Lauder was a popular music hall performer of the early 20th century, famous for his kilt and songs such as 'Stop Yer Tickling, Jock!' as well as his corkscrew-shaped stick.

64 La Pasionaria Memorial
The fight against fascism

Of the many hundreds of statues in Glasgow, only three represent women who are not Queen Victoria. One is Isabella Elder, who ran a shipyard, another Mary Barbour, who organised a rent strike. The third is Dolores Ibárruri from the Basque country, better known as La Pasionaria, the inspirational Republican propagandist of the Spanish Civil War. Her famous stance of *¡No Pasarán!* ('They shall not pass') was chosen as the image for this memorial to the 534 British members of the International Brigade who died in the fight against Franco's fascist forces from 1936 to 1939.

Scotland sent more volunteers per head of population than any other country in the world to join the Brigade. Of the 134 Scots killed, 65 were from Glasgow. They went out of a moral duty to save the world from fascism and, for some, with a sense of adventure. They endured the harsh reality of war in the bloody battles at Jarama, Belchite, Brunete and the Ebro. As the Republican side faced defeat, the International Brigades were disbanded and sent home. During a final parade through Barcelona, Dolores Ibárruri said of them, 'You go with pride. You are history. You are legend.'

In 1974, the International Brigade Association commissioned sculptor Arthur Dooley to create the memorial. It was not erected until the end of 1979, partly because of Dooley's struggle with the small budget of £3000 (which among other things forced him to make it from fibreglass rather than bronze), but also due to a small civil war that broke out at Glasgow City Council. The council had donated £4000 to install the statue by the River Clyde. But a combination of Conservative and Scottish National Party councillors voted to ban it, and La Pasionaria lay neglected in a shed. After the *Glasgow Herald* ran a series of articles on this insult to those who had died fighting for democracy, the statue was finally put in place without ceremony. In 2010, it was restored and rededicated with appropriate honours.

Address Custom House Quay, Clyde Street, G1 4JJ | Getting there Short walk from Central Station; subway to St Enoch | Tip The song 'Jarama Valley', written by International Brigade volunteer Alex McDade from Glasgow, became the anthem of the British Battalion. It may be heard at the traditional music sessions on Sunday evenings at the Dram! pub, 232–246 Woodlands Road.

BETTER TO DIE ON YOUR FEET THAN
LIVE FOR EVER ON YOUR KNEES – Dolores Ibarruri La Pasionaria

THE
CITY OF GLASGOW
AND THE BRITISH
LABOUR MOVEMENT
pay tribute to the
courage of those
men and women
who went to Spain
to fight Fascism
1936 - 1939
2,100 VOLUNTEERS
WENT FROM BRITAIN,
534 WERE KILLED,
65 OF WHOM CAME
FROM GLASGOW

65 The Lighthouse

Mackintosh and the wings of a dove

A good way to start on the trail of Glasgow's most famous architect is to visit the building that was his first major commission. Charles Rennie Mackintosh was low in his firm's pecking order when in 1893 he was given a role in the design of new offices and print works for the *Glasgow Herald* newspaper. He nevertheless managed to leave his trademark style on the stonework and wrought-iron detail. The building is now The Lighthouse, Scotland's Centre for Design and Architecture and home to a permanent exhibition on Mackintosh. Though not rich in artefacts by the architect, artist and designer known affectionately as Toshie, it succeeds in making a collection of model buildings, documents, sketches and photographs into a compelling narrative on his life and works.

A well-illustrated timeline wall takes visitors through his practical education at Allan Glen's School, his 11 years attending evening classes at Glasgow School of Art – an institution he was later to make immortal by his design – and his relatively short but fruitful career as a highly original architect. It chronicles bad times, when depression and heavy drinking affected his work, and happier times, painting at Port Vendres in the south of France, where he and his artist wife Margaret MacDonald went on holiday and stayed for four years.

The Lighthouse took its name from its mission to be 'a beacon for the creative industries in Scotland', and the transformation of the old newspaper works is certainly a shining example. Walk up the 135 steps of the magical spiral staircase inside Mackintosh's tower to get a bird's-eye view over the city roofscape. With birds still in mind, visit the Doocot (Dovecot) Café, in what was once the *Glasgow Herald's* pigeon loft. Imagine if you can the days before telephones, when the latest news and football results came winging in via these feathered friends.

Address 11 Mitchell Lane, G1 3NU, +44 (0)141 276 5365, www.thelighthouse.co.uk | Getting there Short walk from George Square or Central Station; subway to St Enoch | Hours Mon–Sat 10.30am–5pm, Sun noon–5pm | Tip The Lighthouse shop has a wide variety of Toshie memorabilia, including souvenir mugs and a watch bearing an early arts magazine cover design, as well as various cushions which might make that £1,435 Mackintosh chair more comfortable to sit on.

66 The Lismore

Gaels blown by the gales of history

This pub should be approached not as mere licensed premises, but rather as a small art gallery and museum that also offers a fine selection of Scotch whiskies, well-kept beers, outbreaks of live music and conversation. The theme of its unique interior décor, inspired by its location in Partick, is the Highland Clearances. This is the name given to the forced eviction in the 18th and 19th centuries of large numbers of the people of the Highlands and Islands of Scotland, who were burnt out of their homes and chased into exile so that the landowners could make money from sheep farming. Too many of the population were scattered to the winds, and settled in Canada, the USA and Australia. Others made the shorter journey to the burgeoning city of Glasgow, and in particular to the burgh of Partick, which became a haven for Gaels.

A run-of-the-mill bar used to occupy the site. In 1997 it was renamed Lismore, after a small Hebridean island, as a statement of intent. Skilled exponents of the crafts of woodwork, wrought iron and stained glass were tasked with creating a traditional Scottish ambience. Dotted throughout are evocative collages featuring everyday items from Highland and Islands life. They are the work of the late Colin Wilson, who specialised in *objets trouvés*, although it has to be said that many of the items had not actually been lost before being purloined in magpie fashion for the sake of art. The design was overseen by Ranald MacColl, a master of many creative disciplines whose psyche is imbued with both the Highlands and Partick, as is evidenced by the dedication of the men's urinals to the infamous memory of those who perpetrated the Clearances.

The Lismore's lively atmosphere is definitely unlike that of a museum, especially at the Tuesday afternoon music sessions, when elderly troubadors gather to dance and sing, often in the style of Frank Sinatra.

Address 206 Dumbarton Road, G11 6UN, +44 (0)141 576 0102 | **Getting there** Buses 2, 3, 8, 17, 77, 89, 90, 372 to Dowanhill Street; subway to Kelvinhall | **Hours** Daily 11am–midnight | **Tip** The Quaker Burial Ground, a place of repose for members of the Society of Friends dating from 1711, is possibly Glasgow's smallest cemetery. It can be found just off Dumbarton Road on Keith Street.

67 __ Lord Kelvin Statue
Putting the heat into the Industrial Revolution

William Thomson, later ennobled to 1st Baron Kelvin, was a 19th-century academic colossus, who advanced science and pioneered its application to industry when Glasgow was a powerhouse of engineering innovation. One of the many achievements of his long career was creating his own temperature scale. He established that absolute zero occurs at 273 degrees Kelvin. How cool is that? If Glasgow seems not too warm at 7 degrees Celsius, take some comfort from the fact that the temperature is actually a whopping 280 in Kelvins.

Thomson, a quintessential Glaswegian scientist and engineer, was born in 1824 in Belfast of Scots-Irish parentage, and moved to Glasgow when his father was appointed professor of mathematics at the university. Young Thomson attended classes there from the age of 10. In his teens he was already writing papers on advanced mathematical theories; at 22 he became professor of natural philosophy. There was more than a hint of nepotism involved, but Thomson proved to be an inspiring teacher. He advised his students, 'Blow a soap bubble and observe it. You may study it all your life and draw one lesson after another in physics from it.'

During his 53 years as professor at Glasgow, Thomson's restless curiosity took him into boundless areas of mathematics, physics, thermodynamics, mechanics and marine engineering. His ingenuity ranged from inventing a non-drip tap to perfecting the transatlantic telegraph cable. He used this for romantic purposes when, as a 50-year-old widower, he fell in love with Fanny Blandy, 13 years his junior and the daughter of a cable company colleague. On his way to visit the family in Madeira he cabled Fanny asking, 'Will you marry me?' She accepted.

Lord Kelvin is in his academic glory in the statue in Kelvingrove Park, beneath the spire of Glasgow University, whose Hunterian Museum has extensive exhibits on his life and works.

Address Kelvingrove Park, just off Kelvin Way opposite Kelvingrove Bandstand |
Getting there Buses 4, 4A, 15, X25A, X76, X77 to University Union, then a short walk
along Kelvin Way | **Hours** Unrestricted | **Tip** The nearby restaurant and bar Stravaigin
does an eclectic range of local and international dishes, with a large choice of wines by
the glass (28 Gibson Street, G12 8NX).

68 The Mitchell Library

Be seduced by Rabbie Burns

In the likely event of pouring rain, or the much less likely event of sweltering heat in Glasgow, the Mitchell Library is a place of refuge. One of Europe's largest libraries, it was originally established in 1877 thanks to a bequest from tobacco manufacturer Stephen Mitchell. The grandly domed five-floor edifice has a wealth of archives and special collections. None is more special than that devoted to Robert Burns, Scotland's national poet, one of the best in the world, with over 5,000 items including original manuscripts, rare editions, artefacts and ephemera. Material from the collection can be viewed on request. Visitors can, for instance, read the words of 'Auld Lang Syne' in the poet's own handwriting while gazing, should they wish, at a cast of his skull. 'Auld Lang Syne' is the most famous song in the world, with the possible exception of 'Happy Birthday to You'. It is sung at New Year, an emotional time when loved ones are remembered. It has brought a tear to the eye in more than 40 movies, including *It's a Wonderful Life* and *When Harry Met Sally*. The song's popularity is all the more remarkable since much of it is written in Scots dialect, as are many of Burns' works. Help is at hand at the Mitchell, as they have translations in almost 40 languages.

There is also an opportunity to learn about the haggis. Burns managed to compose a paean of praise to this rustic dish that consists of a sheep's heart, lungs, liver and other entrails minced and stuffed into its stomach. His 'Address to the Haggis' is recited with a mixture of solemnity and satire at annual Burns Supper celebrations.

Romance is to the fore in the Burns Collection. He wrote of his love being 'like a red, red rose that's newly sprung in June'. And of a 'fond kiss' that was a 'farewell for ever'. Rabbie, as he is affectionately known, put his romantic notions into practice, fathering 12 children by 4 women, while remaining, of course, true in his heart to his dear wife Jean.

Address North Street, G3 7DN, +44 (0)141 287 2988, www.glasgowlife.org.uk | Getting there Buses 3, 17, 77, X76 to Granville Street; train to Charing Cross | Hours Mon – Thu 9am – 8pm, Fri & Sat 9am – 5pm; contact specialcollections@glasgowlife.org.uk to arrange to see items from the Burns Collection | Tip Haggis is a dish available in many Glasgow restaurants, generally served with mashed neeps and tatties (turnip and potatoes). Veggie haggis is a tasty and healthy alternative. Blaggis, a hybrid of haggis and black pudding (blood sausage), may be an offal offer too far.

69 Mosesfield House

Where cars became a religion

Mosesfield is named after William Moses, an 18th-century merchant whose business was making sedan chairs. By a strange coincidence, the small mansion house in its parkland setting later became the birthplace of the Scottish motor car industry.

By the 1890s, Mosesfield had become the residence of the minister of Springburn United Presbyterian Church. George Johnston, the minister's son, turned the Mosesfield outhouses into a hub for technology. Young Johnston had studied engineering at Glasgow University and caught that institution's bug for invention. He worked in Springburn's railway locomotive industry, but his passion was the internal-combustion horseless carriage. In 1895, he became Scotland's earliest motorist, when he purchased a Panhard car from the continent. Johnston did not know how to drive, and the car was brought from Leith docks to Mosesfield by train and horse-driven wagon. He later committed Scotland's first motoring offence, when he was arrested on Buchanan Street in Glasgow for the then illegal activity of driving after dark.

Johnston formed the Mo-Car Syndicate and set about building the first Scottish car. With investment from industrialist Sir William Arrol, the Arrol-Johnston motor company went into production in 1896 with the six-seater, wood-bodied 'Dogcart'. But his enthusiasm was not matched by commercial success. Ousted from Arrol-Johnston, he set up the All-British Car Company, which ended in liquidation and personal bankruptcy. An attempt to get into the tramcar industry ended when his steam-driven prototype burst into flames on its trial run.

He left Glasgow in 1910 to head West Mexican Mines Ltd, where he pioneered new methods of ore extraction. This also failed financially. Johnston returned to Scotland, and remained an interested observer of the automobile scene until his death in 1945, at the age of ninety.

Address Springburn Park, Belmont Road, G21 3AZ | Getting there Buses 71, 71A, 72, 87, 88, 88A, 88C, 128 to Belmont Road | Hours Mosesfield House is now used as a club for the elderly, and can only be viewed from the outside | Tip An original Arrol-Johnston Dogcart can be seen at the Riverside Museum (100 Pointhouse Place, G3 8RS, beta.glasgowlife.org.uk).

70 Mr Ben Retro Clothing

Dedicated followers of fashion

This is not so much a second-hand clothing emporium as a giant dressing-up box for adults. If, for instance, you want to look like a sentry outside Buckingham Palace in full Scots Guards uniform, complete with busby (the big bearskin hat), Mr Ben is the go-to place. There are many other military options available – dashing red jackets from a variety of regiments, loads of khaki and cosy flying jackets. A green French army greatcoat dating from 1780 is the most antique item in the collection. Away from the battlefield, there is no end of choice of apparel and accessories, from ripped denim and sneakers to dandy vintage frock coats and Britain's biggest collection of top hats. Quality counts, as can be seen in the range of Harris tweed jackets. Most customers come looking for outfits that could be described as ordinary, except that extraordinary and colourful tend to be the norm. Though you may spot the occasional Glaswegian looking like a pirate from the Caribbean, most of Mr Ben's more exotic costumes usually go out on hire for theatre, film and opera productions. Rock musicians flock there to dress on the wild side.

Mary Ann King and her husband Robert Corlett opened Mr Ben 25 years ago, before retro became so fashionable. 'Our customers – mostly young, some slightly vintage – create their own look,' she explains. 'They don't want to be labelled, though they will buy a designer label at a knock-down price.' Mary describes a recent example of a young woman who turned herself into a punk Cinderella, going to the ball in a gorgeous silk gown, an American GI battlefield tunic and a pair of Doc Marten boots.

It is not entirely accurate to describe Mr Ben as a second-hand shop. Much of the stock has had a lot more than one previous owner. Customers come back and trade in the old, maybe for the even older, in a dedicated following of their own fashion.

Address Kings Court, 101 King Street, G1 2RB, +44 (0)141 553 1936,
www.mrbenretroclothing.com | Getting there Buses 2, 60, 60A, 61, 64, 240 to
Candleriggs | Hours Mon & Tue 12.30–6pm, Wed–Sat 10.30am–6pm,
Sun 12.30–5.30pm | Tip The Italian Centre on John Street, Ingram Street
and around has a large number of top fashion designer shops, including Armani,
Boss and Cruise, to use just the first three letters of the alphabet.

71 The Mural Trail

From blight to beauty

Like many a post-industrial city, Glasgow has had its share of urban blight. Add in mindless vandalism and graffiti, and the results were not too pleasing to the eye. The eventual response of the city council was to encourage and even fund highly skilled artists to turn derelict eyesores into eye-catching outdoor art. The city now has scores of gloriously illustrated walls by Smug, Rogue-One, Klingatron and others who are in demand worldwide.

Many of the murals are in a dramatic photorealist style. The gable end of a tenement – often created by the wilful demolition of a perfectly good adjacent building – provides the best canvas for this new breed of city muralists. One in Mitchell Street is decorated with *Honey, I Shrunk the Kids*, Smug's stunning take on the Disney movie. But any stretch of wall or boarded-up shopfront will do.

Animals and birds feature prominently, with local wildlife including the rabbit, badger, fox, robin and deer. There's also a magnificent tiger and a scary crocodile, and a surreal scene with an elephant seated in a pub, a shark with a cocktail and a rhinoceros as bartender. Strathclyde University has turned the exterior of what is perhaps the ugliest building on its campus into the Wonderwall, a vast portrait gallery celebrating the institution's proud history as a leading centre in science and technology.

Most of the murals on the trail are in the centre, but there are many others across the city. There is a delightful and very tall giraffe grazing on a gable end in Shettleston Road, slightly off the beaten track in the East End. Glasgow characters also take pride of place, most notably its favourite son Sir Billy Connolly, comedy genius, film actor, storyteller, writer – and not too bad a singer, despite his insistence on playing the banjo. Given the transitory nature of Glasgow's city centre development, some murals inevitably disappear. Others appear in their wake.

Address The mural trail is available to download at www.glasgow.gov.uk/citycentremurals. It begins at John Street, with Rogue-One's *Hip Hop Marionettes*. | Getting there John Street is a short walk from George Square and Buchanan Bus Station | Tip If you prefer to view your art indoors, you will be spoilt for choice at Trongate 103. This arts centre houses a variety of creative spaces including Glasgow Print Studio, Sharmanka Kinetic Theatre and Street Level Photoworks (103 Trongate, G1 5HD).

72 The Necropolis
John Knox keeps a beady eye on the city

This hilltop cemetery with its extravagant mausoleums and tombs is often described as a city of the dead. A walk along its meandering pathways reveals the Necropolis to be more of a celebration of the lives of its residents, many of them merchants, industrialists, scientists and artists who made Glasgow great. The Necropolis was opened in 1833 as a refined resting place. The required standard of architecture was set by The Bridge of Sighs at the entrance.

Many memorials reflect the wealth rather than eminence of the deceased. The grandest mausoleum, that of Major Archibald Douglas Monteath, was inspired by the Church of the Holy Sepulchre in Jerusalem. The major made his money in the British looting of India – a significant part of his fortune, it is alleged, came from the theft of an elephant-load of precious gems from a maharajah. William Rae Wilson, whose mausoleum is an impressive domed oriental structure, spent his inherited wealth journeying through Palestine, Egypt and most countries of Europe, becoming a learned and popular travel writer. Some smaller memorials are worthy of attention. A Celtic cross for the city's chief constable Andrew McCall was one of the first works of Glasgow's most famous architect Charles Rennie Mackintosh, whose father was superintendent of police. The gravestone of James Henry Alexander, actor-manager of the Theatre Royal, is suitably decorated with a stage and proscenium arch.

John Knox dominates atop a massive column, which predates the cemetery. As 'the Chief Instrument under God of the Reformation in Scotland', he led its transformation into a Protestant country. Knox keeps a beady Presbyterian eye on the city, particularly Glasgow Cathedral, which his zealous followers were intent on demolishing stone by stone. Common sense finally prevailed against the magnificent building being destroyed in the name of religion.

Address Castle Street, G4 0UZ, +44 (0)141 287 3961, www.glasgownecropolis.org | **Getting there** Buses 19, 19A, 38, 38B, 38C, 38E, 57, 57A to Glebe Street | **Hours** Daily 7am–4.30pm | **Tip** Glasgow Cathedral is packed with history, from St Mungo's tomb, through glorious medieval architecture, to the brilliance of its more modern stained glass. Guided tours are free but a donation is welcomed (Oct–Mar, Mon–Sat 10am–3.30pm, Sun 1–3.30pm; Apr–Sept, Mon–Sat 9.30am–5pm, Sun 1–4.30pm).

73__The Old Savings Bank

Art and history set in stone

This hidden jewel of late Victorian architecture once occupied a prime site on the main thoroughfare of the bustling district of Anderston. It now stands isolated amidst modern developments and slightly disfigured by a brick addition. The handsome A-listed rich red sandstone tenement was built in 1889 for the Savings Bank of Glasgow. This thrifty financial institution provided funds for architect James Salmon Junior and sculptor Albert Hemstock Hodge to create a richly decorated work of art, with historic and heraldic references to St Andrew and St Mungo and allusions to Glasgow as a place of industry and commerce. Celtic inscriptions, angels and flora are thrown in for good measure.

One of its intriguing features is a medallion depicting a wise fellow clutching a bag of money, and raising a finger to his temple as if to advise financial caution. The man is Henry Duncan, the founder of the savings bank movement. Born in 1774, Duncan was studying at St Andrews University when his family sent him to Liverpool to work in a bank. But the world of commerce was not for him, and he went on to study for the ministry at Glasgow University. When he was given his own parish, he turned his attention to practical methods of relieving poverty in his rural congregation. He organised a food bank, and created employment for many parishioners. Then he came up with the concept of a bank to help ordinary folk survive hard times. This initiative by a boy who did not want to be a banker grew into the nationwide Trustee Savings Bank.

The Savings Bank, now home to a graphics and web design company, is a reminder of old Anderston, a weaving village which effectively became a proud industrious town in its own right within the city. In the 1960s it was comprehensively 'developed' out of existence, its heart buried under the M8 motorway that separates it from the city centre.

Address 752 Argyle Street, G3 8DS | Getting there Bus 2 to Elderslie Street, then walk through a maze of housing developments; train to Anderston from Central Station | Hours Viewable from the outside only | Tip Nearby at 652 Argyle Street, G3 8UF, Two Fat Ladies at the Buttery is an upmarket restaurant in an enduring and much-loved setting (+44 (0)141 221 8188, twofatladies.com/buttery).

74_ The Òran Mór Ceiling
Many shades of Gray

In 2003, when entrepreneur Colin Beattie was transforming an aban-doned kirk into an enterprise with food, drink, art and entertainment, he sought the opinion of artist and writer Alasdair Gray on what co-lour to paint the huge ceiling. Gray climbed up a ladder, but was not content with just a few strokes. It became obvious that he had de-signs on something much bigger. This was life imitating literature: in Gray's acclaimed epic novel *Lanark,* his character Duncan Thaw paints the ceiling of a Glasgow church. The £6 million budget for the Òran Mór (Gaelic for 'big song') was already strained, but Beattie is a not a man to halt an artist in full flood, and funds were found. A sprightly septuagenarian, Gray spent much of the next decade up scaffolding with his trusty collaborator, artist Nichol Wheatley, cre-ating a heavenly work of art that eventually covered part of the walls as well as the entire ceiling.

The former Presbyterian church now has a ceiling that is often compared to the Sistine Chapel's. Gray's theme, 'a small Scottish model of the universe', careers through a distinctive take on the signs of the zodiac and then veers towards scenes from Scottish town-scapes. The exhortation 'Work as if you live in the early days of a better nation' is based on a poem by Dennis Lee. Medieval imagery mixes with Arts and Crafts and science fiction. It really is life, the universe and everything. The approach is not anti-religious. Carved heads of leading figures of the Protestant Reformation decorate pil-lars on the walls. Martin Luther, John Calvin and John Knox gaze up at the phantasmagorical ceiling and down at the revelry below. Gray and Wheatley have respectfully burnished their names in gold leaf. Colin Beattie seconded this recognition of the history of the old church in a modern way, by adorning the spire with a large pink halo.

Gray's ceiling is in a function suite that is only open for weddings and other events, but a polite request will usually grant access.

Address Byres Road, at junction with Great Western Road, G12 8QX, +44 (0)141 357 6200, www.oran-mor.co.uk | **Getting there** Buses 6, 6A, 10A to Kersland Street or 8, 8A, 90, 372 to Botanic Gardens; subway to Hillhead | **Hours** Daily 11am–3am | **Tip** Òran Mór is home to A Play, a Pie and a Pint, a lunchtime theatre phenomenon that presents 40 new plays, pantomimes and musical dramas a year – and yes, the pie and pint are included in the ticket price (Mon–Fri 1pm, www.playpiepint.com).

75 Pinkston Watersports
Surf in the city

White-water rafting is a pursuit usually associated with a fast-flowing river in a rural setting. But this exhilarating sport is available in the heart of Glasgow.

The Pinkston Watersports Centre also offers a full range of facilities for 'paddlers', the term used to describe enthusiasts of all watersports that involve a paddle. (These should not be confused with the paddlers who kick off their flip-flops at the seaside and go for a gentle stroll in shallow surf.) Among the paddle sports to be enjoyed at Pinkston are fun-yaking – charting choppy waters in an inflatable two-person kayak; river bugging, which involves hitting the rapids in an inflatable armchair; and white-water rafting, a fun family experience. Beside the artificial white-water course there is a 100-metre stretch of calm water, for learning or improving kayaking skills and playing canoe polo. It is also used for open swimming, should you happen to be training for a triathlon. Equipment for all the various sports is supplied.

Glasgow's inner-city watersports centre exists thanks to the initiative of the agency Scottish Canals in putting stretches of the old canal system to modern recreational use. The basins were dredged and rebuilt, with filter systems installed to provide water suitable for bathing. A power of work was involved in cleaning up the formerly neglected waterways, otherwise kayakers would be slaloming around discarded supermarket trolleys.

Pinkston Watersports is located in Port Dundas. The term 'port' gives a clue to how important canals were in Glasgow's industrial growth in the late 18th and early 19th centuries. The whisky distilleries, chemical works, textile mills and iron foundries that once abounded near the canals are gone, some of them now converted into canal-side apartments. A stroll along the waterway past Spiers Wharf shows the potential for more regeneration.

Address 75 North Canal Bank, G4 9XP, +44 (0)141 332 5636, www.pinkston.co.uk |
Getting there Subway to Cowcaddens, then a 12-minute walk; go through the
pedestrian tunnel under the M8, cross Craighall Road on to North Canal Bank and
head towards the orange tower | Hours Mon–Sat 9am–5pm (until 10pm if booked
in advance) | Tip Wakeboarding and paddle boarding are available at Glasgow Wake
Park, which operates out of Pinkston Watersports (+44 (0)7415 787260,
www.glasgowwakepark.com).

76__ The Piping Centre
Wrestle with the bagpipes

If you'd like the opportunity to grapple with the Great Highland Bagpipe, book a place on the Meet the Piper Tour at the National Piping Centre. Properly and sweetly played, the bagpipes are uplifting and potentially addictive, though your first close encounter with this instrument, with its inflatable body and five leg-type appendages, may seem like wrestling with an octopus, and the sound you produce similar to that of an animal in distress. The practice chanter provides a more tuneful introduction. Once you've tried, you may well be tempted to sign up for more lessons. The Piping Centre offers courses at all levels for all ages (and junior-sized pipes for children are available).

The former church in which it is housed is worth a visit in its own right. Built in 1872, the Old Cowcaddens kirk has hints of Greece, Tuscany and Rome, tempered internally with Scottish Presbyterian simplicity. The building's conversion to the home of piping was celebrated with three new stained-glass windows, which reflect in visual terms the history, beauty and complexity of the *Piobaireachd*, a classical form of bagpipe music unique to Scotland. Two of these allude to the landscapes and seascapes of Scotland, which have inspired numerous pipe tunes. The third is about the bagpipe on the battlefield. Generations of Scottish soldiers sought glory but more often found death to the sound of regimental pipers. The war window features a fiery cross summoning clansmen in 1745 to fight for Bonnie Prince Charlie and the Jacobite cause, to wrest the British crown back from the Hanoverians.

The museum has a range of exhibits from the National Museum of Scotland's collection of piping artefacts, including Prince Charlie's own set of pipes. Lamentably, after the defeat of the Jacobite army, all bagpipes (not just Charlie's) were banned, along with wearing the kilt and speaking the Gaelic tongue.

Address 30–34 McPhater Street, G4 0HW, +44 (0)141 353 0220, www.thepipingcentre.co.uk |
Getting there Buses 6, 6A, 10A to Rose Street; subway to Cowcaddens | Hours Mon–Fri
9am–5pm, Sat 9am–3pm (Oct–Mar 9am–noon). See website for information on Meet the
Piper tours, Come and Try workshops and other courses | Tip Take a stroll down to La Boca
at 189 Hope Street, probably Glasgow's most authentic spot for Spanish food and wine. You
might think there's no connection with piping, but bagpipes are popular in northern Spain,
especially Asturias and Galicia.

77 The Police Museum
All about the polis

This fascinating collection of artefacts from over 200 years of police history was put together by former police officers, who also take turns to be on duty, imparting information to visitors on constabularies both local and international. It's great: the public get to interrogate the polis. 'Polis', it should be explained, is Glasgow dialect for police. And as you will see in the museum, *polis* is also the word for police in Swedish and Turkish. You may already know that from watching Nordic noir on TV (though probably not from any Turkish equivalent).

The main feature is the story of Glasgow's own police force. Various city watch agencies funded by the local council had been set up in the 18th century. But in 1800, the Glasgow Police Act established the United Kingdom's first official police force. It predated the Met in London by 29 years, and set the model for other towns and cities. A Glasgow merchant was named Master of Police, in charge of three sergeants and six constables.

The museum displays the changing uniform of the Glasgow polis through the ages. In 1825, it was an elegant tailcoat with top hat. The familiar police helmet had yet to be invented. Among the many colourful and exotic examples of official headgear in the displays from around the world is a cute fez favoured by Libyan cops.

The bobby on the beat in 1825 carried a cutlass for self-defence. Strangely enough, for the Glasgow 'ned' – a Scottish term for a person with criminal and usually violent intent – the sword remained a weapon of choice well into the 20th century. Another piece of historic equipment is a noisy wooden device called clappers, used by officers to summon back-up from colleagues – the origin of the phrase 'to run like the clappers'. This was, sensibly, later superseded by the more strident police whistle. The museum is free and funded by the efforts of volunteers.

Address 30 Bell Street (first floor), G1 1LG (press button 1/1 on door entry system), +44 (0)141 552 1818, www.policemuseum.org.uk | Getting there Buses 2, 60, 60A, 61, 64, 240 to Candleriggs | Hours Apr–Oct, Mon–Sat 10am–4.30pm, Sun noon–4.30pm; Nov–Mar, Tue 10am–4.30pm, Sun noon–4.30pm | Tip Guy's Restaurant & Bar, round the corner at 24 Candleriggs, G1 1TD, is sassy and vibrant, with tasty cuisine.

78 The Pollok Park Highland Cows

Country estate in the city

Probably the most endearing welcome you can get to this city is an inquisitive stare, through a mop of ginger hair, from one of the furry Highland cows that literally belong to Glasgow. These cutest of beasts can be seen roaming the fields of Pollok Country Park, only a short train ride from the city centre. In 1966, when the Maxwell family donated their ancestral 146-hectare estate to Glasgow Corporation, six Highland cows came as part of the deal. The fold – the correct term for a herd of these particular cattle – now numbers around 70. The pedigree Pollok cattle are fine examples of the ancient, hardy breed. One of their number, Una Ruadh by name, was crowned Scotland's bovine beauty queen when she was named champion at a recent Royal Highland Show. The Highlander comes equipped with two furry coats and thrives in a cold, wet climate. When encountered on a dinner plate, the meat is lean, succulent and low in cholesterol.

The park is also home to the Clydesdale, a breed of tall and majestic horse evolved over centuries for heavy work on the farms of Lanarkshire. Compared to their ancestors, these Clydesdales have a more relaxed lifestyle. Visitors can sometimes get up close to them, watching them being groomed and getting fitted with new shoes. In the school holidays, children can enjoy horse-and-cart rides through the park.

There is almost too much to be enjoyed at Pollok Park, and one visit may not be enough. Take woodland walks, check out the wildlife garden, stroll along the White Cart Water with its beautiful arched bridge, explore the formal and walled gardens of Pollok House mansion or just have a picnic. The fairy dell and dinosaur fossil features will enchant children. More active pursuits available include mountain biking and orienteering.

Address 2060 Pollokshaws Road, G43 1AT, +44 (0)141 287 5064, www.glasgow.gov.uk | **Getting there** Buses 3, 49, 57, 57A, 103, 366 to Christian Street; train to Pollokshaws West from Central Station | **Hours** Accessible 24 hours; check website for details of events and attractions | **Tip** In the heart of the park is Pollok House, grand ancestral home of the Maxwell family, preserved and run by the National Trust for Scotland. Among its contents is a fine collection of Spanish paintings. Life below stairs can be explored, and the kitchen is now a delightful tearoom (Mar–Jan, daily 10am–5pm; charges apply). The Burrell Collection museum, also in the park, is currently closed for refurbishment; it will reopen in 2020.

79 _ PS Waverley

A cruise like no other

A day trip on PS *Waverley*, the last seagoing paddle steamer in the world, is an all-consuming assault on the senses. It is not just the scenery and fresh sea air on trips 'doon the watter', round the isles of Bute and Arran, with stops at the Firth of Clyde towns of Greenock, Dunoon, Largs and Helensburgh and on to Tighnabruaich on the Cowal peninsula. The star of the show is the vessel herself, saved from the scrapyard nearly 45 years ago when some 'steamer dreamers' (aficionados of elderly steamships) paid £1 to assume ownership and the task of preservation.

The beating heart of the 239-foot *Waverley* is its engine room, and standing next to the rhythmic pumping of gleaming machinery at full steam is a visceral experience. The din is tremendous as the 2,100-horsepower triple-expansion engine delivers propulsion with a clattering slap. The impossibly shiny rods and rockers, the lovingly polished brass pipes and dials, the immaculate gantry and rails all provide a feast for the eye. You feel the vibrations rising through your feet and the heat from the boilers warming your face and hands. The smell of hot oil fills your nose, and the dings and dongs of the telegraph system ring in your ears as the engineer gets his instructions from the bridge. The effect is mesmeric.

Among the refreshment options on board is the Malt Whisky Bar on the lower level, where the churning vortex of water created by the massive paddles can be seen through the portholes. Regular *Waverley*-goers call it the Laundrette.

Rothesay, a favourite holiday resort for well over a century, was once a sort of Glasgow-sur-Mer, with tenements, tramcars, theatre, winter gardens and many boisterous pubs, all in the glorious setting of the Isle of Bute. The gents' toilets at the pier have been restored to their pristine 1899 condition, and are truly one of the wonders of world lavatorial heritage.

Address 50 Pacific Quay, G51 1EA, +44 (0)141 243 2224, www.waverleyexcursions.co.uk | Getting there Buses 23, 23A, 23B, 26, X19 to Pacific Drive | Hours The *Waverley's* season runs from late May to mid Oct; see website for full timetable | Tip The *Waverley* goes away for some autumn dates cruising in England. You can still travel to Rothesay then, by rail from Central Station to Wemyss Bay, then Caledonian MacBrayne ferry (www.calmac.co.uk).

80 Queen's Park

Sad tale of a golfing widow

Mary, Queen of Scots is one of the most tragic monarchs in history. Her father James V dies a week after she is born in 1542. At the age of one, she becomes queen of a Scotland divided by rebellion and religious war. At age five she is sent to France for her safety, and eventually to marry the heir to the French throne. At age 15 she becomes Queen of France. Two years later she is widowed. She returns as queen to an even more divided Scotland. Her second husband is murdered. Her third husband dies a horrible death in prison. She is deposed as queen by her illegitimate half-brother in favour of her infant son, who becomes James VI. She fights a losing battle to regain her crown, is imprisoned in England, and has her head chopped off.

Despite all her trials and tribulations, Mary managed to fit in regular games of golf. The game could be said to be her downfall. She was spotted playing a few holes at St Andrews only days after the murder of her husband Lord Darnley, and became a notorious golfing widow, suspected of being party to his demise. It seems appropriate that if you take a walk in the park on the site of the Battle of Langside, the ignominious rout that settled her fate, you can do so with golf club in hand.

Queen's Park is one of Glasgow's loveliest, greenest places, with wonderful views from its highest point. One of its many impressive features is its pitch and putt course. This game has advantages over a full round of golf. At Queen's Park it is free to play, with clubs and ball provided, and no booking is required. You only need two clubs. Best of all, it takes a lot less time. Your round of pitch and putt should not last much longer than the 45 minutes it took the queen's inept generals to lose the Battle of Langside in 1568. You can then have a look at the nearby memorial column, erected 300 years after Mary's death, but be careful as it is on a busy roundabout.

Address Langside Avenue, G41 3DJ, +44 (0)7827 305365, www.glasgowlife.org.uk |
Getting there Buses 4, 4A, 5, 312 to Langside Road; train to Queen's Park; the pitch
and putt course is to the east of the park, near the Langside Road entrance | Hours
Park: unrestricted; Pitch and putt: May–Sept, Mon–Thu 11am–9pm, Fri–Sun
11am–6pm | Tip Court Knowe, the hill to the south in Cathcart from where Mary
watched the battle, also has a poignant memorial stone.

81 Rottenrow Gardens

From here to maternity

A small haven of peace in the heart of the city, the Rottenrow Gardens occupy a hillside location within the University of Strathclyde campus. Those of a horticultural bent will appreciate the wild flowers, lilies, geraniums, wisteria, Virginia creepers and ornamental grasses. The remnants of a Victorian arched entrance and portico, plus a pergola with a view and what appears to be a modern take on a Roman arena may have visitors wondering what this place is all about. The clue is in the giant steel sculpture of a safety pin, or nappy pin, to be more exact. (Members of the disposable nappy generation should ask granny to explain.) The gardens are on the site of the Glasgow Royal Maternity and Women's Hospital, where legions of Glasgow babies were born between 1860 and 2001. The artwork, by George Wyllie, is called *Monument to Maternity*.

The institution, founded in 1834 as Glasgow Lying-In Hospital and Dispensary, became better known simply as the Rottenrow, after the busy old thoroughfare where it was located from 1860. The name means either 'road of kings' or 'road of rats'. It definitely had more rats than royals in the 1950s, when its slum tenements were demolished to make way for the campus.

Rottenrow, the hospital, was where the science (and art) of ultrasound in obstetrics was developed. Ian Donald, Professor of Midwifery, pursued the idea that sonar could be used for medical as well as industrial and military purposes. His first investigations in the 1950s involved using a metal flaw detector at a local engineering works, to examine lumps and cysts removed from his patients. Professor Donald was dismissed by some as a crank, but his work soon provided startling diagnostic successes. Countless families have had Professor Donald and his team to thank for successful births – not to mention all those treasured ultrasound pictures of baby still in the womb.

Address Between Montrose Street and North Portland Street, G1 1RQ | **Getting there** Short walk from George Square or Buchanan Bus Station | **Tip** Many of the late artist George Wyllie's works were ephemeral installations. An exception is the Clyde Clock, a very solid metal timepiece on legs, indicating how tempus fugit, or time flies. It is to be found nearby at the entrance to Buchanan Bus Station on Killermont Street.

82 Rouken Glen

Go with the flow

It is not exactly the mighty Niagara Falls, but this picturesque water-fall is just one of many good reasons to visit Rouken Glen Park. There is something pleasantly contemplative about watching the waters of the Auldhouse Burn splash and snake down the rock face. Even on this relatively small scale, the forces of nature are in evidence. The natural falls were enhanced over the years to provide water power for the mills and textile works that operated in Rouken Glen from the 16th century. The Glen Walk from the falls criss-crosses the burn through dramatic gorges, stunning rock formations and steep hillsides. It is a truly great walk. For more gentle perambulation, the 143-acre park has many flatter green areas, including a tranquil walled garden.

Rouken Glen was recently voted UK Park of the Year. It has been a cherished destination since 1906, when the land was gifted to the city. The tram system was extended out to the park, and the citizenry flocked to escape their gritty and polluted daily surroundings. Boating on the large pond (still available in the summer) was a favourite diversion. In 1984 the city, short of funds but not short of parks within its boundaries, leased Rouken Glen to the local East Renfrewshire Council. New ventures, including a butterfly garden, have been added. The Boathouse coffee bar and restaurant is a major success, the quality of food and service matching its splendid setting.

The glen is home to some extraordinary geological features, and part of it is now a designated Site of Special Scientific Interest. Of particular note are the quaintly named Orchard Beds, layers of sandstone and limestone filled with fossils of ancient sea creatures. This exceptional landscape was shaped some 325 million years ago, when the Rouken Glen area was on a coastal plain near the equator, washed by a shallow tropical sea.

Address Rouken Glen Road, Giffnock, East Renfrewshire, G46 7UG, +44 (0)141 638 4121, www.roukenglenpark.co.uk | Getting there Buses 38, 38A, 38B, 38C, 38E or Stagecoach 4 to Rouken Glen Park; train to Whitecraigs from Central Station | Hours Unrestricted | Tip If you cannot get enough of greenery, try Greenbank Gardens in nearby Clarkston. This 2.5-acre walled garden is within the grounds of a Georgian house run by the National Trust for Scotland (Flenders Road, G76 8RB; garden open daily 10am – 4pm, admission charge).

83 Royal College of Physicians and Surgeons
Medicine through the ages

This forward-looking institute of healthcare professionals has been careful to keep records of its considerable past. Visitors are welcome at its historic home to browse through four centuries of Glasgow's contributions to medical progress.

The story begins in the late 16th century when Peter Lowe left Scotland, where there were no medical schools, to study surgery in Paris. He rose through the ranks and became surgeon to King Henry IV of France. He returned to his native Glasgow in 1598 and was appointed town surgeon. A year later the Scottish King James VI granted a charter to Lowe and his fellow doctors and apothecaries to create a 'Facultie of Chirurgeons and Physitians' to organise and improve medical care in the west of Scotland.

The college's library and collections of medical equipment chart Glasgow's role in innovative medicine from Lowe to the present day. Some of the earlier tools of the profession – knives and saws for amputations, a tonsil guillotine – are quite alarming, as are the chisels for brain surgery. These were used in 1879 by William Macewen, when he performed the first-ever successful removal of a brain tumour, saving the life of a 14-year-old girl. The operation benefitted from the pioneering work in antiseptics carried out in Glasgow by Joseph Lister.

David Livingstone, the millworker who became a missionary in Africa, gained his medical qualifications through the college. The collections include the pocket instrument case that he took on his African explorations and a cast of his humerus, which shows the wound inflicted when he was mauled by a lion. On a lighter note, there is a collar presented in 1883 to Sankel, a retriever dog who performed tricks around Glasgow pubs to raise money for the Eye Infirmary.

Address 232–242 St Vincent Street, G2 5RJ, +44 (0)141 221 6072, www.rcpsg.ac.uk | Getting there Bus 2 to Douglas Street | Hours Mon 2–5pm or by appointment: email library@rcpsg.ac.uk | Tip You will want to eat well after your visit, and Martha's at 142A St Vincent Street promises healthy options that miraculously include a black pudding and streaky bacon roll. More exotic choices include chipotle chicken, beetroot falafel and salmon and avocado egg pot (Mon–Fri 7.30am–6pm).

84 Safe Hands Barbers

Cutting edge humour

You might think twice about entering premises with a frankly scary mural of a pair of scissors embedded in a skull adorning its front-age – especially to have your hair cut. And you may not consider it reassuring that the motto of the barber shop in question is: 'Don't worry. It grows back.' Fear not. It is just a highly developed case of Glasgow humour. Daryl Gillespie is the young man responsible. 'Barber shops can be quite boring and predictable places,' he explains, 'but only if you allow that to happen.' The skull and scissors motif was painted by Smug, the Australian-born graffiti artist responsible for many of the great murals in Glasgow. He came up with the idea of the skull, but it was Daryl who asked him to stick in the pair of scissors.

The previous shopfront design was a cheerier affair inspired by Sailor Jerry rum, which sponsored Safe Hands. Not many barbers are prepared to associate themselves with strong drink. And only craftsmen confident of their skills with scissors and razor could get away with the cheeky approach of Daryl and his colleagues. He is very nearly a hairdresser by appointment to the royal family. When Daryl was even younger and very short of cash, he was able to set up his own business thanks largely to the advice and financial aid he got from the Prince's Trust, the youth charity founded by Prince Charles.

These days many Glasgow barbers do not just cut hair, but offer gentlemen's grooming. They have gone all serious and retro. The barbers themselves have compulsory facial hair, with beards like those of King George V and his cousin Tsar Nicholas II, though thankfully not the alarming moustache of his other cousin Kaiser Wilhelm II. Safe Hands is modern, lively and different. Be aware that some of the stylists' banter may involve high jinks, and even low jinks. The conversation is likely to be earthy rather than dull.

Address 5 Miller Street, G1 1EA, +44 (0)141 249 9952, www.safehandsbarbers.com |
Getting there Short walk from George Square or Central Station | Hours Tue–Sat
10am–6pm, Sun & Mon 11am–4pm | Tip Pop into Paesano at 94 Miller Street for
an authentic Napoletano pizza (no reservations).

85 The Saracen Head

A taste of the Gallowgate

One of Glasgow's oldest pubs, The Saracen Head originally opened in 1755 as a coaching inn. The building was largely constructed of stone taken from the ruins of the Bishop's Palace at the nearby cathedral. In Presbyterian Glasgow there was no use for bishops, but a big demand for good-quality building material.

The inn was an elegant establishment, with 36 rooms and stabling for 60 horses. It catered for the merchant class, judges and lawyers, academics from the university and visitors to Glasgow travelling by stagecoach. It boasted: 'The beds are all very good, clean and free from bugs.' At the door stood two waiters with embroidered coats, red plush breeches, and powdered hair, 'to welcome the passengers to the comforts inside'.

Dr Samuel Johnson, the London literary figure, and his biographer James Boswell took rooms during their tour of Scotland in 1773. Dr Johnson is reputed to have had a boozy and fractious encounter here with Adam Smith, the Glasgow academic who went on to achieve fame as an economist and author of *The Wealth of Nations*. Robert Burns visited when he was a struggling young poet, trying (and failing) to persuade a Glasgow company to publish his works. As Glasgow grew, the inn lost its pre-eminence, and was turned into shops and accommodation for the 'humbler classes'.

The Saracen Head survives as an atmospheric – if a little rough-and-ready – authentic Gallowgate pub, known affectionately as the 'Sarry Heid'. It became famous, verging on infamous, for purveying very strong alcohol – champagne cider and fortified wines – to the drinking classes. The ensuing hangovers led to its alternative nickname, the 'Sorry Heid'.

The pub has its own little museum, with artefacts such as the reputed skull of the last witch to be burnt in Glasgow, which are entertaining although they may not stand up to authentication.

Address 209 Gallowgate, G1 5DX, +44 (0)7947 545696, www.saracenhead.com |
Getting there Buses 2, 60, 60A, 61, 240, 255 to Ross Street | Hours Sat from 11am,
Sun from 12.30pm, also open when Celtic FC have home matches; phone to check |
Tip Boteco do Brasil at 62 Trongate is a different kettle of fish, with oven-baked cod
and a mix of prawns and calamari on the menu. Add cachaca cocktails and the sounds
of the favela, and Rio comes to the Merchant City.

86 Scotland Street School

Trepidation in the classroom

More than a century of education is chronicled in the museum housed in this fine old school building. Atmospheric displays include three classrooms reconstructed as they would have been in different eras. A highlight of its regular activities is a session with the stern teacher 'Miss Baxter' (ma'am), who re-enacts the strict discipline of Victorian times. Today's children who attend her classes learn a valuable lesson: schools in those days resembled penal institutions. It all starts in a jolly enough fashion, with dressing up in period costume and being supplied with an educational tool similar in size and shape to an iPad, though it is made of slate and you write on it with a crayon.

Then the discipline kicks in. Sit up straight, feet flat on the floor, arms folded unless told to put hands on head, do not speak unless spoken to, look ahead only. Serious crimes such as putting your crayon into something called an inkwell would incur punishment with a thick leather belt, which ma'am demonstrates with some gusto (by hitting a desk, not a pupil).

Reciting multiplication tables is a simple, quite enjoyable task, but there follows an introduction to the old British monetary system of shillings, pennies, halfpennies and farthings. Even more difficult is the mental arithmetic test, with questions such as how many farthings there are in fourpence halfpenny. At the end, when ma'am explains that she has only been acting, many of the class still look as if they are worried about 'getting the belt'.

Scotland Street School was architect and designer Charles Rennie Mackintosh's last assignment in Glasgow. Its baronial-style towers of leaded glass bring in floods of light. There are gems of Mackintosh artistry to be enjoyed in many corners, although the Glasgow School Board prohibited the full exposition of his unique decorative style, for budgetary reasons.

Address 225 Scotland Street, G5 8QB, +44 (0)141 287 0500, beta.glasgowlife.org.uk/ museums | Getting there Buses 89, 90, 121 to Scotland Street; subway to Shields Road | Hours Tue–Thu & Sat 10am–5pm, Fri & Sun 11am–5pm | Tip The Fish People Café beside Shields Road Subway is a top class restaurant with a wide variety of quality produce, thanks to the fact that the owners are fishmongers (+44 (0)141 429 8787, www.thefishpeoplecafe.co.uk).

87 — Scottish Football Museum

Home of the beautiful game

Scotland's national football stadium, Hampden Park, was the world's biggest until the Maracana in Rio de Janeiro was built in 1950. Hampden still holds records for match attendances in Europe. The official crowd figure for the Scotland v England international in 1937 was 149,415, but an estimated further 20,000 fans found their way into the ground. The stadium is also the home of Queen's Park FC, a small amateur club, but one with a unique history.

Queen's Park is Scotland's oldest team, founded in 1867. Football historians (and not just Scottish ones) have recorded how the club changed the face of the game as we know it. In its early days, the sport was played in a kick and rush fashion, with mobs of players pursuing the ball up and down the park. The Spiders, as Queen's Park became known because of their black and white hooped jerseys, were the first team to develop the tactical passing game that soon became the standard in Scotland and England, and gradually the rest of the world. In the world's first international match, Scotland v England in 1872, the entire home team was made up of Queen's Park players.

All this history and much more is on display at Hampden's Scottish Football Museum. Check out the massive sculptural tableau commemorating one of the best World Cup goals ever, Archie Gemmill's mazy run through the Holland defence in Argentina in 1978. (Scotland won that game, but exited the tournament in yet another glorious defeat.) See the penalty spot stolen from Wembley Stadium in 1977, when Scotland supporters invaded the pitch to celebrate their 2–1 victory over England, and took home the goalposts and much of the turf as souvenirs. Read the original team list document, with Puskas, di Stefano and Gento of Real Madrid, when the Spanish club beat Eintracht Frankfurt 7–3 in the legendary European Cup final of 1960, at Hampden Park.

Address Hampden Park, Mount Florida, G42 9BA, +44 (0)141 616 6139,
scottishfootballmuseum.org.uk | Getting there Buses 5, 6, 7, 7A, 12, 31, 34, 90 to
Hampden Park; train to Mount Florida or King's Park from Central Station | Hours
Mon–Sat 10am–5pm, Sun 11am–5pm; opening restrictions on match days – phone
to check | Tip Partick Thistle, Glasgow's third football team, offer a civil and courteous
alternative to the torrid rivalry of Celtic and Rangers. The 'Jags', who are based at
Firhill Stadium and prefer to be known as Maryhill's premier club, compensate for
their gentlemanly reputation by having football's scariest mascot, Kingsley (ptfc.co.uk).

88__ The Single End

Must-see at the People's Palace

When Glasgow was growing as an industrial powerhouse in the 19th century and attracting immigrants by the hundreds of thousands, the housing shortage became chronic. For many, the only option was a 'single end'. This is what today we would call a studio apartment, where all aspects of daily life – cooking, eating, sleeping, washing – take place in one room. But the difference between a modern-day bachelor pad in Manhattan and a Glasgow single end of Victorian days could not be more stark. These single ends accommodated entire families, with sometimes more than ten people occupying a space suitable for one or two at most.

The People's Palace museum of social history contains a typical single end, reconstructed using original material to show how it would have appeared in the 1930s. For Glaswegians of a certain age, peering into this remembrance of times past would, to use an old saying, bring a tear to a glass eye. Many will remember visiting their grannies in similar single ends in the 1950s. The heart of this small home was the kitchen range, on which a pot of tea stewed to a treacly thickness. A *pot au feu* of Irish stew simmered over the coal fire. There was a sink where everything was washed, from dishes to clothes to small children, usually in cold water. A tin bath filled with warm water could be pressed into service, but that would not be a daily or even a weekly occurrence.

There was one bed, recessed into a wall, where as many as six would sleep, literally head to toe, nose in close proximity to a sibling's feet. A preferred option might have been to sleep on a mattress on the floor. For further discomfort, the communal WC (or 'stairheid cludgie') was located on the stairway, and shared with neighbouring families. In a crowded tenement there was often a queue waiting outside. As compensation, even on a cold winter's day, the seat was usually warm.

Address People's Palace, Glasgow Green, G40 1AT, +44 (0)141 287 0788, beta.glasgowlife.org.uk/museums/venues/peoples-palace | **Getting there** Buses 18, 64, 263 to Green Street or 2, 40, 60, 61, 240, 255 to Bain Street | **Hours** Tue–Thu & Sat 10am–5pm, Fri & Sun 11am–5pm | **Tip** After a thorough examination of Glasgow's social history, a visit to the museum's cosy Winter Gardens café is compulsory for a cup of tea and a scone or three.

89 The Sixty Steps

Upwardly mobile in the West End

Rome has the majestic Spanish Steps; Glasgow has the sturdy Sixty Steps. They might have been called the Greek Steps in honour of Alexander 'Greek' Thomson, Glasgow's second most famous architect, whose trademark was to include Graeco-oriental flourishes, which the steps certainly have. Thomson spent his working life bringing ancient Greece, Egypt and Italy to Glasgow, though he never travelled abroad. A further irony is that the first recipient of a travelling scholarship set up in Thomson's name was a young Charles Rennie Mackintosh, who went on to become Glasgow's most famous architect and designer.

The Sixty Steps were commissioned in the 1870s by John Ewing Walker, a big wheel in the city's lucrative hansom cab trade, whose land straddled the steep gorge carved by the River Kelvin. What could have been a pedestrian bit of civil engineering is instead a treasure trove of classical revivalism, studded with architectural embellishment. But it seems that Walker was more interested in property speculation than art. The Sixty Steps, with their adjacent curved retaining wall and connecting bridge, were strategically located to block access to a rival housing development.

Controversy of an esoteric nature continues, with a debate as to whether Thomson actually did design the Sixty Steps. Some say the rough nature of the stairs and wall is simply not his style. The Greek Thomson Sixty Steps Preservation Trust disagrees. The Belle Vue, a small 'pleasure garden' at the top of the stairs certainly has 'Greek' written all over it. There is a view across the river, to the right of some modern apartments, and when the trees have shed their leaves, of the gable and cupola of an old anatomy building once used by female medical students. It was partly designed by one Charles Rennie Mackintosh, not long after returning from his Thomson travelling scholarship.

Address Kelvinside Terrace/Queen Margaret Road, G20 6DB | Getting there Buses 8, 8A, 90, 372 to Botanic Gardens or 6, 6A, 10A to Kersland Street, then walk up Queen Margaret Drive and Queen Margaret Road | Tip Great Western Terrace is a fine example of Alexander 'Greek' Thomson's work. It is a 15-minute walk from the Sixty Steps, through the Botanic Gardens and west along Great Western Road.

90__ Springburn Park
Decline and fall of a proud community

In 1945, when many cities in Europe were beginning the work of restoration and undoing war damage, the town planners of Glasgow came up with a cunning plan. The answer to the problem of over-crowding was to knock down almost the entire city and rebuild it in a uniform modern style. The Bruce Plan, named after city engineer Robert Bruce, recommended the demolition of much of Glasgow's grand Victorian architecture, including Kelvingrove Museum, the School of Art, the City Chambers, Central Station and the Royal Infirmary. This particular lunacy did not come to pass, mainly be-cause of the costs involved. But the worst excesses of the plan were inflicted on many areas, as tenements were bulldozed and citizens scattered to soulless peripheral estates, or lodged, battery-hen style, in tower blocks.

A visit to the inner-city district of Springburn reveals how a community can be brought to its knees. In its day, it was home to the world's biggest chemical works and Europe's biggest manufacturer of railway engines. But instead of fixing its slum housing and attempting to manage industrial downturn, the decision was taken simply to raze 85 per cent of vibrant Springburn to the ground. The most vicious wound was a huge dual carriageway punched through its heart for the benefit of commuters from wealthier suburbs.

Springburn Park provides a metaphor for this decline. Created as a sumptuous place of recreation at the end of the 19th century, it was funded largely by the Reid family, who owned the locomotive works. Now its Winter Gardens lie derelict, with promises of restoration unfulfilled. Only a fragment remains of the grand terracotta Doulton fountain. The bandstand is gone. The boating pond has no boats. Mosesfield House (see ch. 69) is rapidly joining their ranks. And the beautiful little museum that used to tell Springburn's proud story has been closed.

Address Springburn Park, Belmont Road, G21 3AZ, www.glasgow.gov.uk | Getting there Buses 71, 71A, 72, 87, 88, 88A, 88C, 128 to Belmont Road | Hours Accessible 24 hours | Tip The park remains an interesting destination for rambling and viewing plants. It has a fine rockery and there is plentiful wildlife.

91 Square Sausage

Scottish soul food

This delicacy defined by its shape – square-section, skinless, sliced sausage – is an essential part of local food culture. It may be served as part of the full Scottish breakfast with bacon, eggs, tattie (potato) scone, a link sausage, black pudding, tomato, baked beans, sautéed mushrooms and toast. For many, however, the humble square (made by shaping the sausage meat in a metal loaf tin) is best savoured sandwiched inside a breakfast roll, which it fits perfectly. Accompanied with an ice-cold can of Irn-Bru, the national soft drink, it is a comfort food that is recognised as an effective hangover cure. But you do not require to have overindulged the previous night to enjoy this breakfast. Some people smother it with brown sauce, a spicy relish that contains tamarind. But a good quality square, already delicately flavoured with nutmeg, coriander, pepper and salt, does not require such embellishment. The meat is usually beef, although pork may find its way in, and rusk is added as a binder. The fat content should not be more than 30 per cent.

It is also known by the more upmarket name of Lorne sausage. The origin of this is unclear. Lorne is a rural district of Argyll that may have been the source of the beef. Another popular theory is that the name came from the 1920s Glasgow comedian Tommy Lorne. It is more likely that it was the sausage that made him famous. It is often referred to simply as slice. There is a lesser variety of sliced sausage, made of pork, which is round. To complete the geometry of the Scottish breakfast, the tattie scone is usually triangular. The square sausage is beloved of Scots exiles, and it is the illegal food import most confiscated at US airports.

You will hear Glaswegians specify a Morton's roll. This bakery's product is indeed tasty and has become iconic, but McGhee's rolls stand comparison. So far, neither the square sausage nor the Morton's roll has been granted Protected Designation of Origin status.

Address Square sausage in a roll is ubiquitous in fast and slow food establishments across the city, including Café Wander, 110 West George Street, G2 1QJ (91a); Gordon Street Coffee, 79 Gordon Street, G1 3SL (91b); Bank Street Bar Kitchen, 52 Bank Street, G12 8LZ (91c) | Getting there 91a: short walk from George Square; 91b: at Central Station; 91c: buses 4, 4A, 15, X76 to University Union | Tip Rose & Grants café and deli at 27 Trongate, G1 5EZ, proudly proclaims itself to be 'home of the famous vegan square sausage'. The spicy soya slice is worlds away from the meaty original, but the veggies love it.

92 The Squinty Bridge
A nickname too far

For many decades, the need for ships to be able to sail up the River Clyde almost to the city centre meant a prohibition on low bridges. With the closure of Glasgow's extensive docklands, the traffic in big vessels disappeared but the north and south banks of the river remained poorly connected. Now, as part of the regeneration of the waterfront, four new crossings have been built. The road bridge across to Govan, opened in 2006, is definitely the star. Its official name is the Clyde Arc, and its soaring arch is one of the great sights of a riverside walk. The Glasgow public decided to call it the Squinty Bridge, because it traverses the river at an angle. Similarly, a futuristic pedestrian link nearby was named the Tradeston Bridge, but the citizenry prefer to call it the Squiggly Bridge due to its unusual horizontal curves.

The Squinty Bridge is at the heart of Glasgow's new entertainment quarter. Amidst the proliferation of modern buildings, look out for two curious red-brick domed structures, one on either bank. These rotundas were built in 1890 as part of an ingenious under-river crossing. They were linked by tunnels, one for pedestrians, another for horses and carts and later motor cars, which were lowered in lifts. The vehicle tunnel was filled in in the 1980s. The pedestrian tunnel still exists but is closed to the public, so eerie walks under the Clyde are sadly no longer possible. The North Rotunda now houses a restaurant and the South Rotunda an office.

Two other crossings nearby connect the Scottish Exhibition Centre site on the north bank with the Science Centre, PS Waverley's berth and the BBC Scotland HQ on the south. These are pedestrian not only in function and design but in name. Bell's Bridge was named after the whisky company that sponsored it, and the Millennium Bridge so-called for obvious reasons. They have not been graced by nicknames.

Address Between Finnieston Street and Govan Road | Getting there Buses 100, 320, 351, 395, X19 to Finnieston Street | Tip The Finnieston Strip on Argyle Street is packed with new and exciting restaurants, some of them expensive. Villa Toscana at 1080 Argyle Street, G3 8LY, is however old-school Italian, unpretentious with budget prices.

93 St Charles' Oratory
Terracotta Jesus

Among Glasgow's many churches are a handful of interesting and inventive examples of the modernist style, commissioned by the Catholic archdiocese in the 1950s and 1960s. These buildings were created by an eclectic triumvirate of architects: Jack Coia, a Catholic immigrant from Italy, Isi Metzstein, a Jewish refugee from Berlin and Andy MacMillan, a local boy with a Highland Presbyterian ancestry. Their collaboration is a fine example of Glaswegian diversity.

The Oratory of St Charles Borromeo in North Kelvinside is, externally, an unadorned structure of concrete, brick and glass. Inside there is an impressive and intellectual exposition of Christian imagery, much of which is the work of the sculptor Benno Schotz, a Glasgow-trained Jewish immigrant from Estonia, who joined the team to decorate the otherwise plain interior. Plain, that is, apart from the Mexican onyx, and Italian and Irish marble, deftly incorporated throughout the brick and concrete.

St Charles is an emotional experience, even for a 'lapsed atheist' (as Isi Metzstein described himself). The outstanding feature is Benno Schotz's *Way of the Cross*, depicting the story of Christ's passion and death in a frieze of large terracotta figures. Schotz used real people as models for the 72 characters in the 14 Stations of the Cross. The women of Jerusalem are members of his own Garnethill synagogue, and Schotz himself is standing beside Jesus in the fifth station. His wife Milly features, as does Isi Metzstein, who is the Roman centurion in the ninth station, when Christ fell for the third time. Coia and MacMillan make appearances, and the then parish priest Father O'Sullivan is in the sixth station. The angel who dangles the church's sanctuary lamp from far above is Betty McCaffer, Schotz's cleaning lady.

The church is open every morning except Saturday, and all are welcome at the services.

Address 1 Kelvinside Gardens, G20 6BG, www.saintcharles.org.uk | Getting there Buses 17, 60, 60A, 61, 318, 345 to Braeside Street, then short walk via Stair Street and Kelvinside Drive | Hours Open for services Mon–Fri 10am, Sun noon | Tip The North Star at 108 Queen Margaret Drive, G20 8NZ, has great food and friendly staff. It won the award for best café at the Glasgow Awards in 2017.

94 St Luke's
Saved by rock 'n' roll

It is all change at St Luke's, especially for the saint. The former church in the East End that still bears his name has been transformed, and was recently voted Glasgow's best live music venue. The saint himself has been rebranded: the author of the Gospel according to Luke, the major contributor to the New Testament, has been portrayed through the ages holding writing implements. In Glasgow he is now depicted wearing headphones, and clutching some vinyl instead of his writings.

Like many a church, St Luke's faced demolition, but it has found salvation in rock 'n' roll and food and drink. The atmospheric performance space still has the old kirk's magnificent stained-glass windows flanking the organ pipes. One features the parable of the Good Samaritan and the other, appropriately, the story of the Woman of Samaria, who was drawing water from a well when Jesus, out spreading the word on a hot day, asked her, 'Will you give me a drink?'

St Luke's benefits from being in the Calton, historically a lively quarter of the city. Caltonians are fiercely proud and proudly fierce. In 1787, the poorly paid Calton weavers organised the first major strike in Scottish history. The military were called in and six weavers were killed. More recently Matt McGinn, the late Calton writer and philosopher, celebrated its legendarily edgy social life in a calypso with the refrain 'Murder, polis, in the Gallowgate'.

The venue's bustling bar and restaurant is called the Winged Ox, a reference to the symbol of St Luke who, like the other three evangelists, is traditionally represented by a winged creature. Luke is the ox, a symbol of sacrifice. The Winged Ox feels as if a little bit of New York has found its way to Glasgow, with its pastrami on rye Reuben sandwiches and other deli fare, cocktails and a vintage Coca-Cola dispensing machine. It is a slice of the Big Apple that is also 'pure Calton pawky (i.e. stylish and cheeky, but in a friendly way).

Address 17 Bain Street, G40 2JZ, +44 (0)141 552 8378, www.stlukesglasgow.com |
Getting there Buses 2, 60, 60A, 61, 240, 255 to Bain Street | Hours Daily noon – midnight |
Tip A monument to the martyrs of the 1787 strike and other relics of the handloom
weavers' community are to be found nearby at the Calton Burial Ground, 309 Abercromby
Street, G40 2DD.

95 St Nicholas Garden

Serenity with a hint of scariness

Glasgow Cathedral and its environs bustle with visitors, but nearby there is a place of sanctuary. Across Castle Street, just behind Provand's Lordship (Glasgow's oldest house) is the St Nicholas Garden. In 1446, Bishop Edward Muirhead set up St Nicholas Hospital to care for indigent elderly men. The building is long gone, but the name lives on. The garden is of recent construction (1995) but its imaginative design and use of materials make it evocative of medieval times without descending into pastiche (unlike the faux Baronial-style building opposite, which houses the Museum of Religion).

Pause to examine the entrance gates with their stylised detail of tree, bird, fish and bell from the Glasgow coat of arms. A decorative panel depicts St Nicholas – not just the inspiration for Santa Claus, but also patron saint of moneylenders and sailors – with coins and a boat. Bishop Muirhead is shown on another panel with a model of the hospital. Mary, Queen of Scots gets a mention, as does the fondly remembered local artist Joan Eardley.

Inside is a physic garden, with a collection of plants and herbs of the types that were used in medieval medicine. At the centre is a knot garden in the shape of a Celtic cross, with water lapping gently from a granite font. A sundial may enable visitors to check if their modern timepieces are accurate.

The garden cloisters with oak benches offer a place of relaxation, although peaceful contemplation may be disturbed by the strange Tontine Heads adorning the walls. These mask-like stone carvings date mainly from the 18th century and once decorated the Tontine Building at Glasgow Cross. Some of the faces look tortured and scary: this might reflect the macabre nature of the tontine financial system, in which a group of members paid into an investment fund and the individual who survived the longest eventually inherited all the benefits.

Address Macleod Street, G4 0RA (access from Castle Street), +44 (0)141 287 4350 |
Getting there Buses 19, 19A, 38, 38A, 38B, 38C, 38E, 57, 57A to Collins Street | Hours
Mon–Thu & Sat 10am–5pm, Fri & Sun 11–5pm | Tip The adjacent Provand's Lordship,
built in 1471 for the chaplain to St Nicholas Hospital, had a chequered post-Reformation
history as a barber's, grocer's and sweet shop, and at one time faced demolition. It is now a
small but engaging museum with 17th-century furniture and various royal portraits (+44
(0)141 276 1625; hours as for St Nicholas Garden).

96 St Peter's Church

Dr Livingstone's tutor and his holy brolly

This is the story of two young men, neighbours who worked in a textile mill in Blantyre, Lanarkshire, in the early 19th century. Both had deeply held religious beliefs that would cause them to travel – David Livingstone to Africa as a missionary, Daniel Gallagher to Rome to study for the priesthood.

Livingstone resolved to study medicine in preparation for his work. To do so he needed to learn Latin. Gallagher, with the benefit of a Catholic education during his childhood in Ireland, became his tutor. Each went on to pursue his calling. Gallagher attended the Scots College in Rome. Livingstone walked 16 miles each Monday from Blantyre to Anderson's College in Glasgow, making the return trip on Fridays to work in the mill and attend Sunday service at his church. Father Gallagher returned to Lanarkshire to tend the needs of a poor immigrant Irish flock, living and working in grim conditions. Dr Livingstone went to Africa and became world famous as an intrepid explorer.

In 1855, while Livingstone was crossing the African continent and naming an impressive waterfall after Queen Victoria, Gallagher set up a parish in the burgh of Partick. Mass was first held in a wooden building previously used to house the victims of a cholera outbreak. So unsuitable was it as a place of worship that a parishioner had to hold an umbrella over Father Gallagher as he conducted services, to protect him from dripping water. It was soon replaced with a stone church, small and neat in early Gothic style, dedicated to St Peter. By 1903, with the exponential growth of Partick's Catholic population, a larger church was required, and a new St Peter's was built, designed by Peter Paul Pugin with magnificent cathedral-like proportions and an elaborate interior. An umbrella, said to be the very holy brolly that protected Father Gallagher, is preserved as an unusual historical relic.

Address 46 Hyndland Street, G11 5PS, +44 (0)141 357 5772, www.stpetersglasgow.co.uk |
Getting there Buses 2, 3, 8, 8A, 17, 77, 89, 90, M4 to Dowanhill Street; subway to Kelvin-
hall | Hours Mass Mon–Fri 10am, Sat 6.30pm, Sun 10.30am, noon; Father Gallagher's
umbrella is not on public display, but may be seen on request (a donation to the roof repair
fund might aid access) | Tip The earlier St Peter's church is called St Simon's. It has a
modern triptych painting celebrating the Livingstone-Gallagher connection (33 Partick
Bridge Street, G11 6PQ, +44 (0)141 339 7618).

97 __ The Subway
Going round and round

It is difficult for passengers to get lost on the Glasgow underground. Unlike that of many cities, its system is not a jumble of interconnecting lines. The Subway is a circle with two sets of tracks, Inner and Outer, running side by side but in opposite directions. Either way they eventually go through the same 15 stations. The old song 'I Belong to Glasgow' describes the city as 'going round and round' after the singer has had a couple of drinks. It may have been inspired by the Subway.

The carriages are small, and run on an unusually narrow 1.22-metre gauge. It can seem like taking a trip on an oversized toy train set. The ride is 'awfy shoogly' – in other words, the carriages shake about vigorously. Children get free entertainment by standing in the aisle without holding on and pretending they are surfing. Adults also surf, but usually when they are on a Subcrawl, which is a group pursuit involving buying an all-day ticket and stopping at all 15 stations to have a drink in a nearby pub. A legendary piece of Glasgow humour relates that whenever Chic Murray, a droll and surreal comedian, travelled on the Subway he would ask, 'Is there a buffet car on this train?'

The Subway dates from 1896 and is the third oldest underground in the world, after those of New York and Budapest. For some reason it serves only the western and southern parts of the city. Though it has been modernised, the many proposals over the decades to extend the system have not come to pass, mostly for financial reasons, but also because of technical issues with the Mickey Mouse size of the trains. The Subway continues to run in splendid isolation from the rest of the city's transportation lines, with the exception of Queen Street and Partick railway stations. Glasgow's population has declined from its one-time peak of 1.2 million to around 600,000 today. The city has shrunk to fit its Subway.

Address See www.spt.co.uk/subway for maps and general information | **Hours** Trains run Mon–Sat 6.30am–11.40pm, Sun 10am–6.12pm | **Tip** The small Jacobean-style building beside St Enoch station, which resembles a cute castle, was built in 1896 as the headquarters of the Subway company. It is now a warm and welcoming coffee shop.

98 Summerlee

Where old tramcars still trundle

The North Lanarkshire town of Coatbridge, a few miles east of Glasgow, is home to the Summerlee Museum of Industrial Life. Based on the site of a former ironworks, it has all sorts of working machinery, as well as a walk-about colliery and mine shaft, and workers' cottages with interiors vividly reconstructed to evoke different eras. It is also the only place in Scotland where you can still ride on a working Glasgow tram.

The golden era of Glasgow's tramway is long gone. More than 250,000 people turned out in 1962 to see the final tramcar journey. There were tears as the city closed a service that not only held a special place in the hearts of its citizens but had also been a spectacular success story. At the turn of the 20th century, the Glasgow tram network was the envy of other nations. It was an egalitarian form of transport; a journey cost one penny for all. Shipyard workers travelled alongside the professional classes on a service notable for its cleanliness, promptness and neatly uniformed crews.

Thousands of tramcars trundled through the streets for 20 hours out of 24. In 1914, the network carried 336.6 million passengers. The junction of Renfield Street and Union Street was held to be the busiest in the world, with 466 tramcars passing per hour on weekdays and 516 on Saturdays. The network extended far beyond the city limits, even out to Coatbridge.

The legacy of the trams lives on. Revenues were enormous, and by 1911 there was a capital surplus of £4 million. The trams were publicly owned, so cash flowed into the city's coffers. With municipal foresight some of this was siphoned into a Common Good Fund, which survives to this day and is used to fund civic ceremonies and hospitality to distinguished visitors to the city. If you are ever invited to a reception at the City Chambers, remember to raise your glass to the memory of the Glasgow tramcar.

Address Heritage Way, Coatbridge, ML5 1QD, +44 (0)1236 638460, culturenl.co.uk/
summerlee | Getting there Train to Coatbridge Sunnyside from Queen Street Station,
then 13-minute walk | Hours Apr–Oct, daily 10am–5pm, Nov–Mar, daily 10am–4pm |
Tip The National Museum of Rural Life has a working farm, tractors, harvesting machines,
lambs, calves and bees. To the south of Glasgow, it can be reached in 40 minutes by bus 31
from St Enoch Centre (Wester Kittochside, Philipshill Road, East Kilbride, G76 9HR,
+44 (0)300 123 6789, www.nms.ac.uk/national-museum-of-rural-life; charges apply).

99 _ Tabac Panther Milk Bar
The little room at the back

Tabac comes under the general heading of style bar, a dark and cool place with reclaimed Parisian street lighting, quirky bits of art and loads of craft beers. The candlelit room at the back could be described as secret, though it is known and appreciated by many. Let's just say that it is not obvious.

It is an unusual concept: take a small storage space. On Friday and Saturday nights, add a few tables and chairs. Don't bother with any normal stuff like décor. Open at 9pm and close at midnight. Serve customers from an old, disused lift in the corner. Offer one drink only: Panther Milk. This is a concoction of milk, condensed milk and various strong spirits. It comes in several flavours: vanilla dusted with cinnamon, mint, coffee, triple sec and grenadine.

Panther Milk (particularly the pink version) may appear to be what is known in Glasgow as a 'woman's drink' but, as the name suggests, it has a bite. *Leche de Pantera* dates back nearly a century, and was the drink of choice for the tough *hombres* of the Spanish Foreign Legion. It was created by a legendary Madrid barman called Budgie at the behest of José Millán Astray, the tough, one-eyed, one-armed commander of the legion and henchman of the dictator Franco. It was a cocktail the legionnaires could whip up with basic ingredients, although you might wonder where they got ice from in the deserts of North Africa.

In the 1970s, Panther Milk was adopted as a cheap and potent drink by trendy young Spaniards, even in the decidedly non-Franco territory of Barcelona. Paul Crawford, founder of Glasgow's SubClub and guru of the nightclub scene, imported the idea from the Catalan capital. The Barcelona Panther Milk bars tended to be basic, hidey-hole places where animated conversation rather than loud music was the norm. This shabby chic ambience has certainly been replicated in the little bar at the back of Tabac.

Address 10 Mitchell Lane, G1 3NU, +44 (0)141 572 1448, www.tabacbar.com | Getting there A short walk from George Square or Central Station; subway to St Enoch | Hours Tabac: daily 11am–midnight; Panther Milk Bar: Fri & Sat 9pm–midnight; booking advisable | Tip SubClub, famous electronic music venue and the world's longest-running underground dance club, is nearby at 22 Jamaica Street (Tue & Thu–Sun 11pm–3am).

100 The Tall Ship
When Glenlee met Mary Doll

The tall ship *Glenlee* is berthed beside the Riverside Museum of Transport. This barque, to give the three-masted, square-rigged sailing vessel her proper maritime designation, was built on the Clyde in 1896, and was something of a rarity in that age of steam. Designed for service as a bulk cargo carrier, SV *Glenlee* glided the oceans for two decades, mainly on trips round the Cape of Good Hope to Australia and back via Cape Horn.

In 1922, she was purchased as a training ship by the Spanish navy and renamed *Galatea*. After nearly 50 years of service, with a short period in the Spanish Republican Navy that included capture by Franco's Nationalist forces, the ship was laid up and left to rot. The Clyde Maritime Trust charity bought the old barque at auction, and thanks to their work the *Glenlee* now sits gloriously restored on Clydeside as a museum ship. During restoration, the Spanish navy kindly donated various parts of the superstructure they had removed and kept in store. The *Glenlee*, as she was renamed on her homecoming, was missing her figurehead of a buxom blonde lady. This was carefully recreated by Scottish carver Marvin Elliot. So proud is Glasgow of the ship that the lady on the prow was nicknamed 'Mary Doll' after a local TV comedy character, the long-suffering wife of Govan philosopher, drunkard and work shyster Rab C. Nesbitt.

It was later discovered that the original figurehead had been kept safe and well at a Spanish naval museum in Ferrol. A polite request for its return to the mother ship did not this time meet with generosity. The Spanish response, allegedly, was that they would hand over their *Maria Muñeca* when Britain gives back Gibraltar.

The Tall Ship is a place for both education and fun. With its handsome interiors and floodlit riverside setting, it is also a popular wedding venue. Bring your own captain to conduct the ceremony.

Address 150 Pointhouse Place, G3 8RS, +44 (0)141 357 3699, www.thetallship.com |
Getting there Bus 100 to Riverside Museum; subway to Partick, then 7-minute walk |
Hours Feb–Oct, daily 10am–5pm, Nov–Jan, daily 10am–4pm | Tip Glasgow's
famous shipping company the Anchor Line ran its ocean liners from the adjacent
Yorkhill Quay. Get a hint of luxury-liner dining at their period head office, now the
Anchor Line restaurant (12–16 St Vincent Place, +44 (0)141 248 1434).

101 Tam Shepherd's Trick Shop

It's pure magic

Tam Shepherd's has been serving practical jokers, magicians and fun seekers from the same location since 1886. This Glasgow institution is where badly behaved children of all ages (some now collecting the state pension) buy their prankster equipment. Favourites include the whoopee cushion, which simulates chronic flatulence, the foam brick for pretending to break windows, and fake plastic vomit (as if there is not enough of the real stuff on Sauchiehall Street on a Saturday night). The small detonators for creating exploding cigars have miraculously survived health and safety legislation.

Sometimes the joke is on you – big ears that turn you into Prince Charles, fangs and blood capsules that bring out the inner vampire. From the wide range of facial hair you may go Scottish with the full ginger set. In the headgear department, the traffic cone hat – as worn by the Duke of Wellington's equestrian statue up the road – has become de rigueur. For the classical look, laurel wreaths are available in green or gold. There is the opportunity to change your persona completely, with one of the large selection of masks. You can become a unicorn, Scotland's national beast, or a cute panda. The werewolf mask might help you fit in at some of the Glasgow pubs that can resemble the Mos Eisley Cantina out of *Star Wars*.

Tam Shepherd himself was a magician by trade, with an impish sense of humour. Current custodian Roy Dalton is still involved at the age of 85 with the shop his family has run for 75 years. He is an expert on card tricks, and his books remain standard texts in the world of magic. You too can try your sleight of hand with the purchase of some vanishing coins, a box of 58 easy-to-learn tricks, or an 'Educated Duck' to do the work for you.

Address 33 Queen Street, G1 3EF, +44 (0)141 221 2310, www.tamshepherdstrickshop.co.uk |
Getting there Short walk from George Square or Central Station; subway to St Enoch | **Hours**
Mon–Sat 10am–6pm | **Tip** The LAB is an interesting pub with a courtyard, hidden up the
lanes between Queen Street and Buchanan Street. So called because it serves up cocktails and
shots in test tubes, it also has beers, wines and grub of a high standard (26 Springfield Court,
daily 11am–midnight).

102 The Templeton Building

A beer with a view

'Gallus' is an adjective often used in Glasgow. It has a range of meanings: stylish, flashy, show-off, bold, cheeky and, in its ancient usage, fit for the gallows. The Templeton family were being gallus in every way when, in 1888, they decided to build an extension to their carpet factory near the Gallowgate. Industrialists in those days liked to exhibit their wealth by creating factories with elaborate exteriors, in stark contrast to the working environment inside.

Architect William Leiper was hired to create a sort of Doge's Palace at Glasgow Green. The result may not be a patch on the awesome original in Venice, but the Templetons did not stint on the enamel tiles and terracotta decorating the red brickwork. They could afford to, having made a substantial fortune with their innovative mechanised methods of producing chenille Axminster carpets, quality products found in many top locations including the House of Commons and the ill-fated luxury liner *Titanic*.

The creation of the elegant façade had a human cost. A contemporary news account detailed a disaster during its construction in 1889, when 'a gale of extraordinary severity caught the wall of the new building, dashing it down through the roof of the weaving shed of the old mill'. Twenty-nine women, some as young as 14, were killed as they worked at the looms. Their names are inscribed at a memorial garden in nearby Tobago Street.

The carpet factory, once Britain's biggest in terms of output, closed in 1979. The building has been carefully preserved, and now houses West, a German-style brewery, restaurant and beer garden, where a pint of St Mungo lager can be enjoyed while admiring the palatial surroundings. Another part of the old factory has been converted into spacious flats – a most gallus address.

Address Templeton Street, G40 1AW; West: www.westonthegreen.com | Getting there Buses 18, 46, 64, 263 to Abercromby Street; train to Bridgeton from Central Station (low level) | Hours West Bar & Restaurant Sun–Thu 11am–11pm, Fri & Sat 11am–midnight; brewery tours available – see website | Tip Glasgow's love affair with the world of beer can be pursued further at the Republic Bier Halle. The centrally located lively basement bar has a varied menu including German sausage and goulash (9 Gordon Street, G1 3PL, +44 (0)141 204 0706).

103 The Tenement House
Come into the parlour

Glasgow has a huge array of tenements, ranging from the splendid to the squalid (though most of the latter have been improved or demolished). The house at 145 Buccleuch Street, Garnethill, built in 1892, comes somewhere in the middle. What makes it unique is that one of its first-floor flats has been preserved, as if in aspic, in virtually its original condition.

Miss Agnes Toward moved here with her widowed mother in 1911, and occupied it for 54 years. After Miss Toward's death in 1975, the landlord was planning to empty the flat and modernise the interior when Anna Davidson, a Glasgow actress, chanced upon it and decided it had to be saved for posterity. She bought the flat and its entire contents, everything from the furniture to Miss Toward's jewellery and personal papers, and even a jar of plum jam dated 1929. Anna spent seven years here before securing the future of this gem, by passing it into the care of the National Trust for Scotland.

Compared to life in a single end (see ch. 88), Buccleuch Street was sheer luxury. The flat had a living room (parlour), bedroom, kitchen and – what bliss – a posh bathroom with a WC, deep bath and hot, running water. There was a bell for summoning a maid from the kitchen, though the Towards did not have a servant. Mrs Toward made a living as a dressmaker, working from home. Agnes worked as a shorthand typist. They took in lodgers, to boost household income.

The furniture is of solid good quality, including a grandfather clock, a rosewood piano and a chest with a large drawer, for storing top hats. The table in the parlour set for afternoon tea, the family portraits, and Miss Toward's many personal accoutrements around the house hint at a modest gentility and a life well lived. The tenement's tiled entrance way is a good, if somewhat plain, example of the great tradition of the 'wally close' (see ch. 33).

Address 145 Buccleuch Street, G3 6QN, +44 (0)141 333 0183, www.nts.org.uk/Visit/
Tenement-House | Getting there Subway to Cowcaddens; train to Charing Cross, then
10-minute walk; see website for directions avoiding steep hill | Hours Apr–Jun & Sept,
Oct, daily 1–5pm, July & Aug, Mon–Sat 11am–5pm, Sun 1–5pm | Tip The Singl-end
Café-Bakehouse round the corner does astonishing cakes, breakfasts, open sandwiches and
other fare too multitudinous to mention. Staff are dog- and human-friendly (265 Renfrew
Street, G3 6TT, Mon–Fri 9am–5pm, Sat & Sun 10am–5pm).

104 Timorous Beasties

Of mice and interior design

It may be a small shop, but inside is an Aladdin's Cave of design that is sought after worldwide. Stylish decorative fabrics, wall coverings and ceramics are at the core. But there is much more to the story of how Alistair McAuley and Paul Simmons, who met in the late 1980s at Glasgow School of Art, have made their unique decorative mark. The name comes from Robert Burns' poem about a field mouse – 'wee sleekit, cowerin, tim'rous beastie' – whose world is overturned by the blade of a plough. At the heart of this design duo's inspiration is the eternal truth that nature and art are inextricably linked.

Their style is far from timorous. Respect for their craft and consummate technical skill are matched with a highly irreverent approach, most famously in their 2004 Glasgow Toile wallpaper. This translated a classic French pattern depicting 18th-century rural life into a gritty and witty urban landscape, featuring a junkie shooting up on a park bench, public urination and other realistic city scenes, all deftly delineated. The prolific output from their studio is to be found in many upmarket suppliers of home furnishings. It has featured on film and TV, including *Sex in the City* and the BBC's *Sherlock*, and been collected by the likes of the Chicago Art Institute, Victoria & Albert Museum and Glasgow's Gallery of Modern Art.

McAuley and Simmons are in constant demand for their collaborative work. They leave a distinctive stamp on any surface that can be printed upon. To name but a few: aeroplanes for Netjet, Penguin book covers, the programme for Kate Bush's comeback concert, Royal Bank of Scotland banknotes, chocolate boxes for Fortnum & Mason, and the smoking room of the Duke of Buccleuch's stately home. Visitors can purchase a cushion or ceramic mug from the wee Glasgow shop, and may be inspired to check out the many wonders available from Timorous Beasties online. It's not cheap, but it is art.

Address 384 Great Western Road, G4 9HT, +44 (0)141 337 2622, www.timorousbeasties.com | Getting there Buses 6, 6A, 10A to Lansdowne Crescent; subway to Kelvinbridge | Hours Mon–Sat 10.30am–6pm | Tip Wintersgill's at 226 Great Western Road is one of Glasgow's grand traditional pubs, with a mixture of Victorian and Art Deco interiors. The locals who go there come in equally diverse styles. Cold beer, a warm welcome, affordable wines and wholesome pub grub are guaranteed.

105 The Titan Crane

The Eiffel Tower of Clydebank

What does a town once famous for building the biggest and most luxurious ocean liners in the world do when its shipyard is closed down and demolished, and its last remnant is the rusty giant of a 46-metre cantilever crane? When the people of Clydebank were asked this question, they voted to preserve the Titan Crane and turn it into a visitor attraction. And so it stands, now gleaming and cherished, and marvellously illuminated at night.

The 800-tonne colossus, the world's first electrically driven crane, was built in 1907. In its restored state the Titan has won a number of engineering heritage awards. But, in its elegant retirement, what is it used for? The Titan has hosted weddings, and a new brand of whisky was launched there. And it obviously has stunning views up and down the River Clyde and across the surrounding hills. The adventurous can abseil down, or bungee down and up, and then down again. Serious thrill-seekers can swing across the river at 70 miles per hour. There is a lift for the saner visitor, who will get enough exhilaration merely from standing on the metal grille of the top deck and looking all the way down. Children like to lie on this floor and pretend they are flying.

But for the young visitor there is also a lot of education going on at the Titan: maths, engineering, geography and especially history. About how Clydebank was known as Tamson's Town, when the Thomson family opened their first shipyard on the rural landscape and built houses for the workers. How the yard then became John Brown's, where Cunard liners such as the *Queen Mary* and many, many battleships were built. How Clydebank rebuilt itself after being virtually destroyed in two nights of saturation bombing during World War II. And how the Clyde shipyard workers faced the threat of closure in the 1970s, not by strike action but by a work-in – carrying on building ships.

Address Queens Quay, Clydebank, G81 1BF, +44 (0)141 562 2889, www.titanclydebank.com | **Getting there** Buses 1, 2, 6, 40 to Clydebank Bus Station; train to Clydebank from Central or Queen Street Stations, then a 10-minute walk | **Hours** Temporarily closed to visitors due to works on infrastructure; reopening Mar 2019 | **Tip** It is only a 25-minute train journey from Clydebank to Balloch, the gateway to the bonnie, bonnie banks of Loch Lomond, for boat trips on Scotland's loveliest loch and country hikes.

106 The University Café

Ice cream and hot peas

In the late 19th century, thousands of Italians fled the rural poverty of their native land and came to Scotland. Many settled in Glasgow where, though the streets were not paved with gold, hard work and initiative could be rewarded. The Scots-Italian community has since made a considerable contribution to the city in the fields of art, architecture, music, theatre, education, law – and of course cuisine.

In the early days, the catalyst for the Italian community was ice cream, initially sold in the streets from handcarts, and then from shops as thrifty families invested in property. By 1905, Glasgow had 336 ice cream parlours. The other staple in the growing Italian café culture was the hot pea special, a dish of marrowfat peas laced with vinegar and white pepper. Fish and chip shops also became an Italian domain, serving affordable sustenance to the masses. Thankfully the shameful days of catering to the local palate by deep-frying pizza have more or less gone, and the city now has a host of high-end family-run restaurants, trattorias and delis offering an authentic taste of Italy.

The number of old-style cafés has diminished, and the University Café is one of the few such institutions to survive virtually unaltered. The interior has changed little since 1918 when it was constructed by Pasquale Verrecchia, an immigrant ship's carpenter who swapped shipyard work for his own café. The ice cream is still made to an original recipe by the third generation of the Verrecchia family. Diplomas in ice-cream excellence from many decades decorate the walls. There is old-fashioned confectionery, memories of when it was a specialist sweetie shop. The menu, from Scottish comfort food to Italian classics, has substantially increased from the old days, but it still serves the traditional hot pea special, and is probably the last place of its kind in the city to do so.

Address 87 Byres Road, G11 5HN, +44 (0)141 339 5217 | **Getting there** Buses 8, 8A, 90, 372, M4 to Chancellor Street; subway to Kelvinhall or Hillhead | **Hours** Mon–Thu 9am–10pm, Fri & Sat 9am–10.30pm, Sun 10am–10pm | **Tip** The Italian Cloister Garden in the grounds of St Andrew's Cathedral is a place of peace, with striking modern sculptures and a 200-year-old olive tree from Tuscany. It commemorates the hundreds of Italian civilians who lost their lives during World War II in the sinking of the Arandora Star. They were being sent into exile when the ship was torpedoed (196 Clyde Street, G1 4JY, www.italiancloister.org.uk).

107 The University Cloisters
Get down to the undercroft

As an exemplar of Gothic Revival architecture, Glasgow University's main building is second only in stature to the Houses of Parliament in London. Its most intriguing and atmospheric space is the undercroft beneath Gilbert Scott's stunning Bute Hall, known as the Cloisters. The newly graduated gather under its archways of fluted columns and ribbed vaults to celebrate with a glass of something fizzy. It is also a place of contemplation, where generations of eminent alumni and visitors have trod, and where in 1933 Albert Einstein famously popped out for a smoke after being given an honorary degree.

The student body has included many who went on to find fame in a variety of fields: two prime ministers, two first minsters of the Scottish parliament, seven Nobel laureates, physicist Lord Kelvin, TV inventor John Logie Baird, iconoclastic psychiatrist R. D. Laing, pioneer of brain surgery Sir William Macewen, actor Gerard Butler, veterinarian and author James Herriot, and Bluebells' singer Ken McCluskey, who topped the charts with *Young at Heart.* Founded in 1451, Glasgow University was located in the High Street until 1870, when it moved away from the overcrowded city centre to Gilmorehill in the leafy West End. The Lion and Unicorn stairway in the quadrangle dates from 1690, having been dismantled and moved stone by stone to be rebuilt in the new location. It connects the university to its earlier famous alumni. The economist and philosopher of the Scottish Enlightenment Adam Smith considered its teaching superior to that of Oxford. James Watt worked there on his steam engines that would fuel the Industrial Revolution. Campaigner for democracy Thomas Muir was forced to leave the university in 1785 because of his radical views, but was not deterred from his zeal for political reform and was eventually banished to a penal colony.

Address University Avenue, G12 8QQ, +44 (0)141 330 2000, www.gla.ac.uk | Getting there Buses 4, 4A, 15, 370, X25A, X76 to University; subway to Kelvinbridge | Hours Visitor information centre at main gate: Mon 9.30am–5pm, Tue–Thu 9am–5pm, Fri 9am–4pm; guided tours available – check website | Tip Eusebi Deli, 152 Park Road, G4 9HB, has everything an Italophile could crave including pinsa, a Glasgow-friendly pizza topped with chips (+44 (0)141 648 9999, www.eusebideli.com).

108__ The Vintage Vehicle Trust

Retirement home for beloved buses

The collections of this de facto museum of transport include a handful of beautifully restored fire engines, and a few retro lorries returned to spick and span condition. But the big passion of the Glasgow Vintage Vehicle Trust (GVVT) is for buses. It is a place of sanctuary for trusty old passenger carriers that were once headed for the scrapyard after years of public transport service. Most of the current tally of 126 vehicles are owned by individual members of the trust, who devote considerable time and money to prolonging the lives of their pet buses.

The GVVT is based at the former bus garage in Bridgeton, a building that has itself been rescued from demolition and oblivion. During the decades when the city was at the height of its industrial power, its teeming population was served by Glasgow Corporation Transport with an almost military rigour. The buses, like the extensive tramway network they gradually replaced from 1925, ran on time thanks to the conductors' insistent refrain of 'C'moan, get aff!' This is Glaswegian for 'Please board and descend from the vehicle as quickly as possible.'

The serried ranks of bright and shiny buses of all ages at Bridgeton have evocative names like the Tiger Cub, Panther, Atlantean, Valkyrie, Leopard, Dominator, Olympian, Javelin and Dart. All are restored meticulously in their original colourful liveries, including the green, white and orange of Glasgow 'Corpy' and the red, cream and green of MacBrayne's.

The GVVT's Back on the Road project means that the grand old buses are often to be seen on the city streets at special events. Much of the work at Bridgeton is done by people who have taken a wrong turning in life, but have found a new social focus in the garage's repair bays.

Address 76 Fordneuk Street, G40 3AH, +44 (0)141 554 0544, www.gvvt.org |
Getting there Buses (naturally) 18, 263 to Bridgeton Station or 64, 164 to Fordneuk
Street; train to Bridgeton from Central Station | **Hours** Open to the public on open
days and for events; check website for details. Members (join for £15/£13) have
regular access, and visiting enthusiasts are usually accommodated | **Tip** The open-top
buses of City Sightseeing, with their knowledgeable guides and drivers, offer an
efficient and entertaining way to get a complete picture of Glasgow. There is an optional
'Ghoulish Glasgow' commentary (daily 9.30am – 4.30pm, +44 (0)141 204 0444,
www.citysightseeingglasgow.co.uk).

109___Wallace's Well
A taste of freedom

'Modest' hardly begins to describe this shrine to Scotland's most famous freedom fighter. But the historic significance of the site, in the northern Glasgow suburb of Robroyston, will strike a chord with proud Scots and, no doubt, fans of the movie *Braveheart*. It was at this well in August 1305 that William Wallace had his last sip of water as a free man.

Despite Wallace's early success in the war of independence, driving out invading English armies, Scotland was again under occupation. Wallace was a fugitive in his own land with a huge price on his head. On his way to Glasgow Cathedral to seek help from Bishop Wishart, a staunch supporter of the struggle, he stopped at Robroyston. Wallace was only one night from the safety of the bishop's castle when he was betrayed by Sir John Menteith, a former ally who had chosen traitor's cash and advancement under English rule. Wallace was captured and taken to London where he was brutally hanged, dismembered, beheaded, and had his heart cut out.

The Wallace Well has been cherished for centuries as part of the local heritage, but largely ignored by the powers that be. In 1970, it was listed for protection as a historic monument. Wallace was betrayed in a different way in 1993 when Historic Scotland deleted it from their list as not being of sufficient interest. Removal of the protected status became a serious issue when the threat emerged of the well being obliterated as part of a housing development.

Public protest ensued. Historians confirmed the authenticity of the well, the Society of William Wallace lobbied the authorities and the kilted warriors of Clan Wallace raised metaphorical broadswords in support. The situation was resolved when the housing developer worked with volunteers to restore and preserve the site. A Celtic cross nearby, dating from 1900, marks the site of the farmhouse where the capture took place.

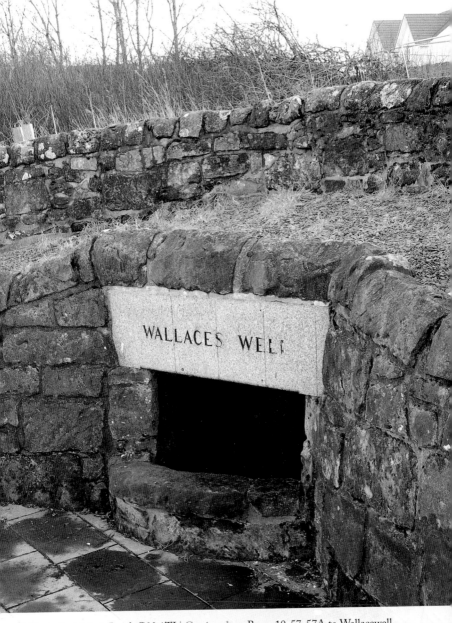

Address Auchinleck Road, G33 1TJ | **Getting there** Buses 10, 57, 57A to Wallacewell Road or McGills 72 to Auchinleck Road from Buchanan Bus Station | **Hours** Unrestricted, but the well is next to a busy country road so it is advisable to visit during daylight hours; see www.robroyston.org for more information | **Tip** The village of Elderslie in Renfrewshire, 11 miles west of Glasgow, is the birthplace of the Scottish hero. He is commemorated by an ancient yew tree and a memorial column, where a ceremony is held every August to mark the anniversary of his execution (see www.thesocietyofwilliamwallace.com).

110_ The Whangie

A walk in royal footsteps

Queen Victoria ruled over an empire upon which the sun never set. You might think, then, that she was never short of a foreign holiday destination. But she chose to be a frequent visitor to Scotland, often indulging her enthusiasm for settings described in the works of Sir Walter Scott. On her journeys north of the border she was apt to take a break to stretch her regal legs, stroll up a suitably sized hill for a wee picnic and take in the panorama. In her wake, locals and cartographers dubbed several of her Caledonian pitstops 'Queen's View'.

Just north of Glasgow, in the Kilpatrick Hills, is one such vista. From the Queen's View car park, the path to Victoria's favoured outcrop is clear to see along a duckboard walkway before it reaches up the hill. A five-minute climb is rewarded with a royal view that stretches over Loch Lomond to the Arrochar Alps and, on a clear day, to the Highlands.

Go further than the queen did and you'll find what lurks beyond, and lures so many walkers and rock climbers. Around 30 minutes further along the trail – stick to the lowest paths for the most direct route – lies the delightfully named Whangie. This unusual craggy formation is a slice of rock that has split from the side of the hill, leaving a narrow ravine 15 metres deep and 90 metres long.

Legend says that the fissure was caused by Satan whipping his tail in excitement as he flew overhead after servicing a witches' coven, en route to another hot date in nearby Strathblane. Without doubting the devilish attractions of Strathblane women, the reality is that the alteration to the landscape was created during the last Ice Age by a phenomenon called glacial plucking. To vary the return route, follow the path out of the crags, stick to the left, and go back via Auchineden Hill, enjoying the fine views over the Campsie Fells, to make a total walk of around 2.5 miles.

Address Accessed from Queen's View car park, A809, nearest postcode G63 9BA | Getting there By car, A809, 30 minutes from Glasgow city centre between Milngavie and Drymen; bus C8 from Buchanan Bus Station (Mon–Sat, limited services, morning & early evening only); keen walkers can take the John Muir Way to Blanefield or Strathblane (about one hour) where there are other buses back to Glasgow | Tip The Carbeth Inn, a famous historic pub near the Queen's View, is being transformed into a café and farm shop.

111 The Women's Library

Feminism, facts and fun

This eminent institution for the celebration and empowerment of women is housed in a building created by architect J. R. Rhind in gorgeous Edwardian Baroque style. It is one of five similar libraries he designed, funded by Scots-American philanthropist Andrew Carnegie, which were sprinkled like jewels across the tenement city.

When the library opened in 1906 it was a segregated space. The gentlemen's reading room was vast, with a much smaller area allocated to women. This was an obvious reason for protest, but women at the time were otherwise engaged in the struggle for the right to vote. Glasgow Women's Library took over the premises in 2013. Under their able regiment the building has been transformed into a warm and welcoming place where all, regardless of gender or age, can enjoy what is not just a lending library but the UK's only accredited museum devoted to women's lives, histories and achievements.

With advance notification visitors can browse the vast archives of documents and artefacts covering an impressive list of subjects, from the stirring history of the suffragette movement and the campaign for zero tolerance of domestic violence, to more homely topics like cookery and knitting.

The library's events spaces are bustling with activities. Exhibitions, films, readings and meet-the-author sessions abound. The written and spoken word is to the fore. Budding authors are encouraged through workshops such as Creative Writing for Fearties (a Scots word for those unsure of their skills). There are Mistress (as distinct from Master) Classes. Jane Austen Day involves readings, afternoon tea and dressing up in period costumes. Burns Night has been marked by a re-enactment of the attempt by suffragettes to set fire to the cottage that was the birthplace of Scotland's macho national poet, Robert Burns. There is no shortage of fun at Glasgow Women's Library.

Address 23 Landressy Street, G40 1BP, +44 (0)141 550 2267, www.womenslibrary.org.uk |
Getting there Buses 18, 46, 64, 263 to Anson Street; train to Bridgeton from Central
Station | **Hours** Mon–Fri 9.30am–5pm, Thu 9.30am–7.30pm, Sat noon–4pm | **Tip**
The Suffragette Oak, on University Way in Kelvingrove Park, was planted in 1918 to
commemorate the granting of votes to women. In 2015, the Women's Library campaigned
successfully for it to be named Scottish Tree of the Year.

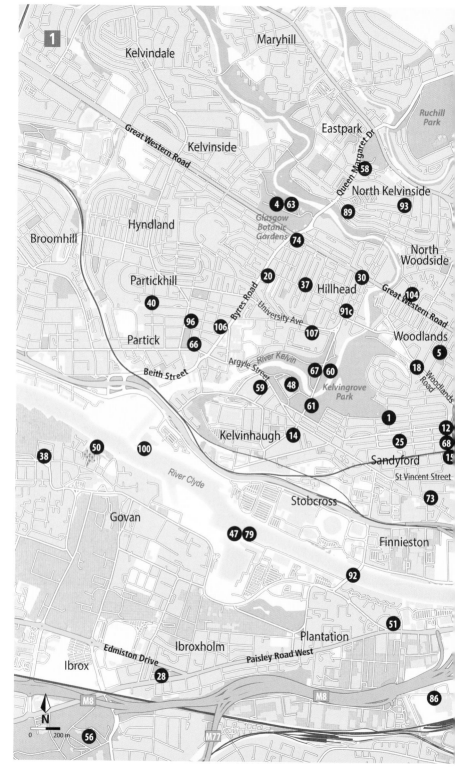

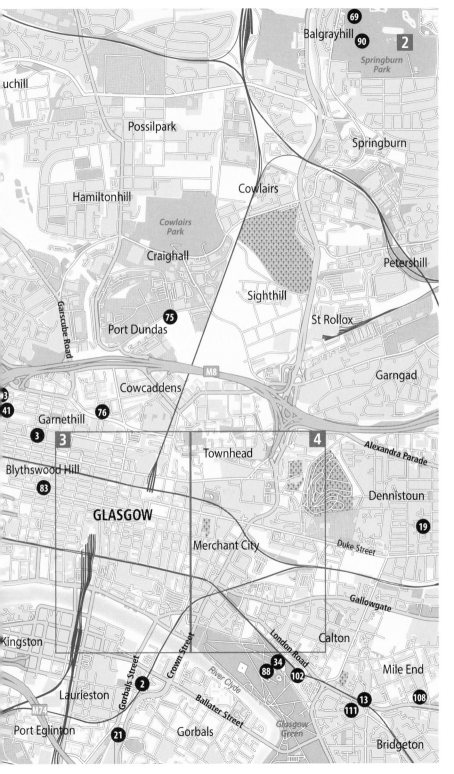

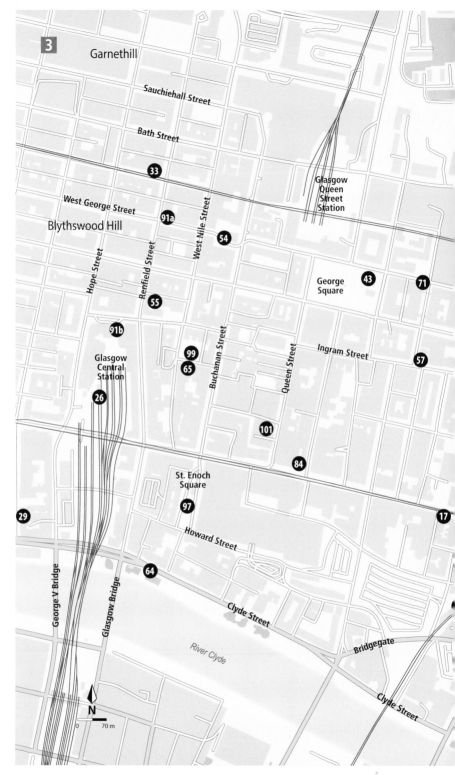

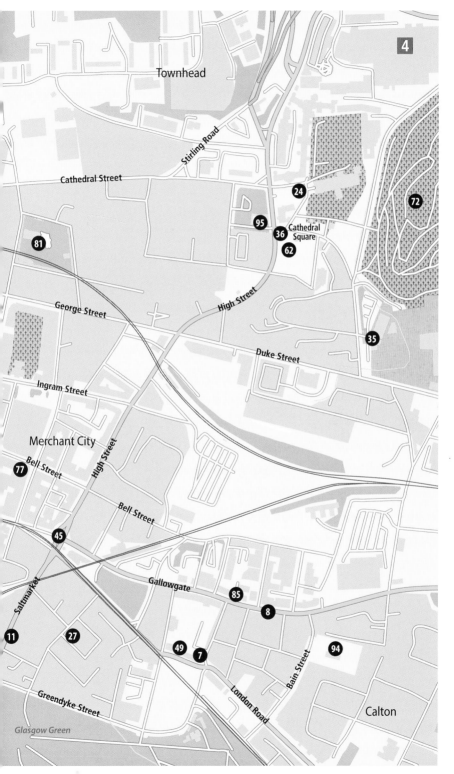

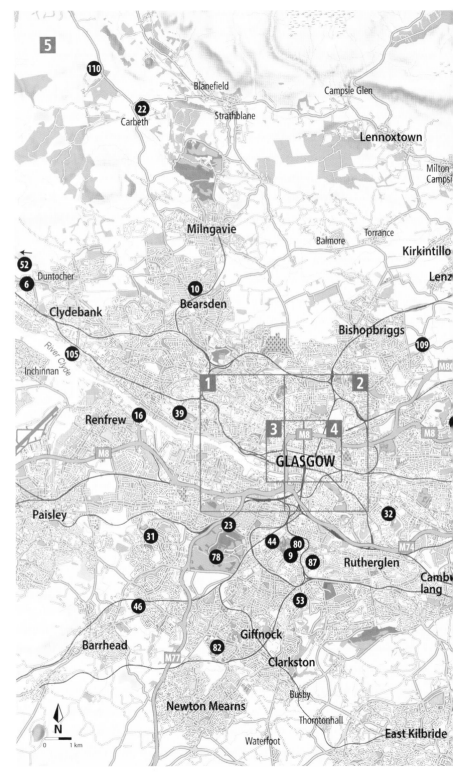

Gillian Tait
**111 PLACES IN EDINBURGH
THAT YOU SHOULDN'T MISS**
ISBN 978-3-95451-883-8

Kirstin von Glasow
**111 SHOPS IN LONDON
THAT YOU SHOULDN'T MISS**
ISBN 978-3-95451-341-3

Jo-Anne Elikann
**111 PLACES IN NEW YORK
THAT YOU MUST NOT MISS**
ISBN 978-3-95451-052-8

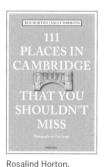

Rosalind Horton,
Sally Simmons
**111 PLACES IN CAMBRIDGE
THAT YOU SHOULDN'T MISS**
ISBN 978-3-7408-0147-2

Rike Wolf
**111 PLACES IN HAMBURG
THAT YOU SHOULDN'T MISS**
ISBN 978-3-95451-234-8

Giulia Castelli Gattinara
**111 PLACES IN MILAN
THAT YOU MUST NOT MISS**
ISBN 978-3-95451-331-4

John Sykes
**111 PLACES IN LONDON
THAT YOU SHOULDN'T MISS**
ISBN 978-3-95451-346-8

Julian Treuherz,
Peter de Figueiredo
**111 PLACES IN LIVERPOOL
THAT YOU SHOULDN'T MISS**
ISBN 978-3-95451-769-5

Rüdiger Liedtke
**111 PLACES IN MUNICH
THAT YOU SHOULDN'T MISS**
ISBN 978-3-95451-222-5

Kirstin von Glasow
111 GARDENS IN LONDON THAT YOU SHOULDN'T MISS
ISBN 978-3-7408-0143-4

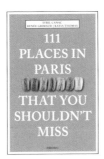

Sybil Canac, Renée Grimaud, Katia Thomas
111 PLACES IN PARIS THAT YOU SHOULDN'T MISS
ISBN 978-3-7408-0159-5

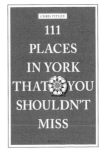

Chris Titley
111 PLACES IN YORK THAT YOU SHOULDN'T MISS
ISBN 978-3-95451-768-8

Nicola Perry
33 WALKS IN LONDON
ISBN 978-3-95451-886-9

Justin Postlethwaite
111 PLACES IN BATH THAT YOU SHOULDN'T MISS
ISBN 978-3-7408-0146-5

Alexandra Loske
111 PLACES IN BRIGHTON AND LEWES THAT YOU SHOULDN'T MISS
ISBN 978-3-7408-0255-4

Frank McNally
111 PLACES IN DUBLIN THAT YOU SHOULDN'T MISS
ISBN 978-3-95451-649-0

Laura Richards
111 LONDON PUBS AND BARS THAT YOU SHOULDN'T MISS
ISBN 978-3-7408-0021-5

Kirstin von Glasow
111 COFFEESHOPS IN LONDON THAT YOU MUST NOT MISS
ISBN 978-3-95451-614-8

Acknowledgements

Thanks to Melanie Stewart, Linda Arthur, Jim Divers, Calum Hind, Lesley Robertson, Una Ross, Sharon Stewart, Douglas Aitken, Graham Shields, David Harding, Stewart Noble, Donald Fullarton, Tom Joyes, Liz Buie, Alastair Ramsay, Mimi Moreni, Tommy Reilly, Marco Giannasi, Rocco Conforti, Karen Pickering, Andrew Lee, Andrew McAinsh, Ron Abercrombie, all the helpful people at Glasgow Life and many others who nominated favourite places and opened doors. A special thanks to Gillian Tait for her detailed knowledge of Glasgow and editorial guidance. Most of all, as visiting rock bands say at the end of their concerts, 'Thank you, Glasgow'.

The Author

Tom Shields was born in Glasgow and has never left, apart from frequent sojourns in Barcelona, which is a fascinating place but not Scottish. He studied at Strathclyde University on and off (more off than on) and after 32 years graduated with a hybrid BA degree in engineering, mathematics, Spanish, Latin American studies, Catalan and wine-tasting. He fell into journalism at an early age, and spent more than 40 years being paid to have fun at the *Glasgow Herald* and *Sunday Herald*, much of the time writing supposedly humorous Diary columns, before escaping into retirement. His Diary books are still bestsellers in charity shops.

The Photographer

Gillian Tait is a native of Edinburgh. She is a Gill-of-many-trades; trained as an art historian and then as a painting conservator, she originally worked in the museum sector. More recently she has occupied her time as a researcher, editor, writer and photographer, while indulging her passions for singing and travel, particularly to Italy. Her first book as both author and photographer was *111 Places in Edinburgh That You Shouldn't Miss*.